Presented by:

Date:

God's Little Devotional Book for the WORKPLACE

eagle
Guildford, Surrey

Originally published by Honor books P.O. Box 55388
Tulsa, Oklahoma 74155.
This edition published 2001 by Eagle Publishing Ltd, PO Box 530, Guildford, Surrey GU2 4FH. British Library Cataloguing in Publication Data. A catalogue record for this book is available from the British Library.

Manuscript written/compiled by Todd Hafer

Typeset by Eagle Publishing
Printed by Cox & Wyman, Reading
ISBN No: 0 86347 415 2

God's Little Devotional Book For the Workplace

Introduction

At work. It's where you spend the lion's share of your waking hours. (And, perhaps occasionally, a few of your slumbering hours as well.) Many people spend more time at the job than they do with their families, enjoying leisure pursuits or snoozing contentedly in their beds.

Consider this: If you begin a full-time, 40-hour-a week career at the age of 22 and retire at 65, you will spend the equivalent of 3,440 24-hour days on the job. That's 9.5 'round-the-clock' years of nothing but work – no holidays or sick time. If you are a salaried professional associate, increase that total by 25 per cent to accommodate your 50-hour work weeks. If you're a small-business owner, increase it by 50 per cent. Research indicates you may well be putting in 60-hour weeks.

What an incredible personal investment! That's why it's so important to glean as much wisdom, joy, laughter, skill and satisfaction as possible on the job. This book is designed to help you do just that. You'll learn about key workplace virtues – perseverance, creativity, diplomacy, efficiency and teamwork. And you'll have a few laughs over the humorous stories you'll read. Many are taken from actual workplace communiques and notices.

We hope you'll appreciate *God's Little*

Devotional Book for the Workplace so much that you'll want to share it with your co-workers.

You work hard for your money. You deserve a book that works for you. We believe you're holding it right now. Read and enjoy.

The difference between ordinary and extraordinary is that little extra.

Let us not become weary in doing good, for at the proper time we will reap a harvest if we do not give up.
Galatians 6:9

An Oregon schoolteacher went to Nordstrom's department store to buy a $1 booklet on how to tie scarves. An assistant told the teacher that, unfortunately, the store had sold out of the item. Four weeks later, the teacher looking through her mail, to her surprise, found two of the booklets, at no charge. That gesture made her a faithful Nordstrom customer, even though they didn't have what she wanted the first time around.

But that's not the whole story. There is no Nordstrom department store in the teacher's home town. She drives a 160 miles round trip to shop at a store that took the time and effort to compensate her because they were out of a simple, inexpensive booklet.

You might not always be able to give customers or co-workers exactly what they want. But the way you go above and beyond to make up for an oversight, mistake or product shortage can build a greater sense of loyalty and satisfaction than if you merely meet the initial request.

What will customers or clients remember about you when you are not able to meet a request? The mere fact that you couldn't provide what they wanted? Or, the creative, service-minded way you responded to the situation and turned a negative into a positive?

A closed mouth gathers no foot.

A fool uttereth all his mind.

Proverbs 29:11 KJV

Stacy, a young college graduate, spent a summer gaining experience at a small publishing company.

Near the end of the summer, the president of the company told Stacy he wanted to talk to her about a full-time job. Stacy excitedly told one of the editors about her upcoming meeting with the president to discuss an offer.

'Stand your ground,' came the reply. 'Don't settle too low.'

A week later, Stacy burst into the editor's office. 'Guess what I'll be making?' she bubbled.

When Stacy blurted out the amount, the editor looked shocked. 'That's more than I make,' she said quietly. 'And I've been here five years.'

The next day, the president summoned Stacy to his office. 'I have something of a revolt on my hands,' he told her evenly. 'It seems that you broadcast your salary, and quite a few of your co-workers are bitter about it. That was confidential information. Now, I'm afraid that we won't be able to bring you on board. There would be too much resentment.'

There are a few things you should never discuss with co-workers: your love life, your medical history and your salary.

If you want to
be original,
be yourself.

Do not neglect your gift.

1 Timothy 4:14

A man who thought he had an amazing replica of a Leonardo da Vinci painting took his work of art to a museum. He showed the copied painting to the curator to get his reaction. The curator immediately identified the painting as a forgery – and also the copyist, his nationality and when the copy was made.

Then the curator turned the painting over. The information on the back confirmed that he was right on all three counts. 'How did you know it was a fake?' the man asked. 'It looks like an amazing likeness to me.'

'People who make a living copying the masters have little imagination of their own,' the curator explained. 'And this person's choice of subject, brush strokes and areas of emphasis practically scream "Fake!" Think about those celebrity impersonators – how they overemphasize a certain vocal inflection or gesture. It's the same thing here.'

If you truly want to distinguish yourself, be an innovator, not an imitator. God has given you unique skills, ideas and experiences. It's OK to be inspired by role models, but use that inspiration to develop your own distinctive style. The world doesn't need a clone of someone else. It needs the one and only you!

To tend unfailingly,
unflinchingly,
towards a goal
is the secret of success.

Let us run with perseverance
the race marked out for us.
Hebrews 12:1

Hank Aaron never led major league baseball in batting average or home runs during any single season. And he struck out more often than almost any other batter. However, when it came to sheer persistence and overall consistency, he was unmatched. He broke Babe Ruth's monumental record of 713 career home runs – and kept right on hitting balls out of the park.

In fact, many baseball experts wonder if his final total of 755 will ever be equalled.

No matter what kind of job you hold, persistence and consistency will help you build a solid reputation as a person who can be counted on to deliver the goods. Consistency, by its nature, isn't something that gets noticed immediately; and it's not always easy to remain focused in today's constantly shifting work environments. But over time, persistence and consistency emerge and shine.

You may see some flash-in-the-pan types grabbing all the attention, but keep hammering away, just as Hank Aaron did. When these folks are gone and forgotten, you will be remembered – and valued.

Learning to leave
some things undone
is incredibly
satisfying.

It is in vain that you rise up early and go late to rest, eating the bread of anxious toil; for he gives sleep to his beloved.

Psalm 127:2 NRSV

Japan's snow monkeys work hard just to stay alive in their frigid habitat. They must climb high mountains continuously as they search for food. Interestingly, however, they take frequent breaks to rest, renew themselves, even monkey around a little. They seem to have an innate understanding that all work and no play leads to exhaustion – and maybe extinction.

Contrast the monkeys to many of Japan's human workers who have literally worked themselves to death. The drive for performance – exemplified, not only by output, but by hours put in – permeates their culture. This tragic syndrome has become so prevalent that it's been given its own name: *karoshi.*

It's sad that those in the monkey business seem to have more sense than those in everyday human business. Like the monkeys, we humans have been instilled with certain instincts that tell us what our bodies, minds and spirits need. Eat when your blood sugar drops – sleep when you're fatigued – seek quiet when the noise of the world sets you on edge – and so on.

Don't kill yourself trying to be top banana at work. Take the time to relax and eat a banana instead.

The place to be happy is here. The time to be happy is now.

The light in the eyes [of him whose heart is joyful] rejoices the hearts of others.

Proverbs 15:30 AMP

According to nutritionist Pamela Smith, one hundred laughs a day provide a cardiovascular workout equal to ten minutes of rowing or biking. Additionally, laughter stimulates stress release the same way exercise does. Laughter also helps fight infection by sending hormones into your bloodstream that cut the immune-weakening effects of stress. Proverbs 14:30 puts it this way: 'A heart at peace gives life to the body.'

Today's work environment, with all its demands and unknowns, can be like a giant pressure cooker. Laughter is the safety valve that lets the steam escape before there's an explosion. Lighten up and loosen up when possible. Laugh at the absurdities of life – your workplace will no doubt provide an almost endless supply of material.

Strive to be a source of laughter on the job and wherever you go.

No limits but the sky.

If you falter in times of trouble, how small is your strength!

Proverbs 24:10

In the late 1950s, the owner of a small chain of general merchandise stores in the southern states of America noticed that he couldn't keep the popular hula-hoops in stock. This craze swept the country like wildfire, and not even the manufacturer could keep up with the demand.

'We're sorry,' the manufacturer told the owner. 'This product has become a nationwide craze, and we simply aren't able to produce our product quickly enough to keep up. You will have to wait quite a while, we're afraid, before you will have more hula-hoops.'

The owner could have told his managers to apologize to customers, then explain that the popular item simply wasn't available. Instead, this man ordered some plastic tubing and began making his own hoops – at the astonishing rate of three thousand a night!

This resourceful, proactive store owner brought the same sense of resourcefulness and can-do attitude to everything he did. He was willing to jump through whatever hoops necessary to satisfy his customers. Eventually, his chain of stores grew to national prominence, and the man became a billionaire. His name? Sam Walton.

Your true character is revealed by what you do when no one is watching you.

I have hidden your word in my heart
that I might not sin against you.
Psalm 119:11

Farmers have a saying that goes, 'Once you're standing in the pig pen, it's a little too late to worry about soiling your Sunday clothes.' And that sound piece of advice carries beyond the farm. The key to avoiding wrong-doing and compromise at work is to decide in advance to stay as far away from it as possible.

Impropriety has a way of revealing itself a little at a time. Once we begin thinking that some form of wrong-doing is 'not so bad', it's often just a few more steps to the pig pen, with little hope of escaping without getting dirty.

Promise God and yourself right now that you will resist even the appearance of wrong whenever you encounter it. Decide ahead of time how you will handle hypothetical situations. Would you lie to a client? Falsify documents? Fudge on your expense report?

Determine what the 'pig pens' are in your job, and don't go near them. Remember that an ounce of prevention can be worth ten pounds of purity.

The world has forgotten,
in its concern with
Left and Right,
that there is an
Above and Below.

Godliness with contentment is great gain.
For we brought nothing into this world,
and it is certain we can carry nothing out.
1 Timothy 6:6–7 KJV

A young man completing a job application came to the line asking for his permanent address.

He began to write his home address, but he paused for a moment. Then, with a small smile, he wrote, 'Heaven'. He understood that heaven is a real place – and the ultimate home of all God's children.

We spend a lot of time at work. (Especially if we're in middle management!) Sometimes it seems like way too much time. You may have found yourself uttering, 'I practically live here!'

But work is not your true home. In fact, even the earth is not your true home. The time you spend on the job is like one tiny dot on a continuous, unending line. Think about that the next time you need to regain perspective.

We will be more conscious of God in our everyday lives if we remember – like the young man – that He is the Landlord of our permanent home. Someday we will actually meet God. How we will feel about that experience depends on how we spend our time on our temporary home – this earth.

Worrying is like paying interest on a debt you might never owe.

'Who of you by worrying can add a single hour to his life?'

Matthew 6:27

It's amazing how minor irritations can take our eyes off God. Tension headaches interrupt our sleep. Telemarketers interrupt our dinner. Car troubles interrupt our holidays. Phone calls interrupt our work. Corporate restructurings interrupt our career goals. Lost overnight packages interrupt our job progress – and sometimes our digestion!

At times like these, we must step back and gain perspective. Will the world stop turning if we don't quite make that deadline or don't get a hoped-for promotion? Will babies no longer smile and birds no longer sing if net revenues don't meet budget – or a less-than-deserving person gets Employee of the Month?

What is a parking ticket or flat tyre or late report or missed deal or cold sore or reprimand from a manager compared with being loved purely and eternally by Almighty God and being made clean from all our sins?

A hit song several years ago advised, 'Don't worry. Be Happy'. Better advice might be, 'Don't worry. Be heavenly'.

The riches that are in the heart cannot be stolen.

Whoever loves money never has money enough; whoever loves wealth is never satisfied with his income.

Ecclesiastes 5:10

Many Americans have a possession obsession. Laptop computers, digital TVs, mobile phones, sports cars – all the 'right' stuff. These items aren't inherently bad, but they can easily become a source of false security, even pride.

The same danger exists with money. It's easy to become obsessed with earning bonuses, enjoying profit sharing, and fattening a 401K account. Remember when the salary you made early in your career seemed like great wealth? Perhaps now you're not satisfied. You'd like to get a substantial raise and get to the next level – the next plateau on Money Mountain.

Life is a journey. We never know what's around each curve, through each forest, across each river. Jesus taught His followers to travel light, taking with them only what they would need for their journey. He reminded them to concentrate on God's divine love. It provides a richness unmatched by any worldly possession. This love is so brilliant that it makes everything else pale in comparison. Materialism, on the other hand, is excess baggage that in the end only serves to make the journey burdensome.

Activity strengthens.
Inactivity weakens.

Do you not know that your body is a temple of the Holy Spirit, who is in you? . . . Therefore honour God with your body.

1 Corinthians 6:19–20

If an esteemed guest, a king or queen or prince, came to live with you, what accommodation would you provide? Would you make your home as clean, inviting and pleasant as possible?

Or would you let rubbish accumulate and let the house go to ruin?

Or what if you knew that the Prime Minister or the President of the United States or some foreign dignitary was coming to visit your place of business? If such a person paid you a surprise visit at work today, how would you feel? Embarrassed? Proud? Ashamed? Disgraced?

The Bible teaches that our bodies are the temples of God's Spirit. Is your temple an appropriate dwelling place for God? Sadly, some people's offices are in a lot better shape than their own bodies.

We don't have to be hard-bodied models or Olympic athletes, but our bodies are gifts from God, and we are to honour Him with them. If you are unsure about the state of your health, take this quick self-test: which do you tend to take two at a time – doughnuts or stairs?

In the end, it's not the size of your pay cheque that matters – it's the size of your dream – and the small steps you take every day to make your dream real.

Who despises the day of small things?
Zechariah 4:10

Our world loves 'bigness'. Large, economy-sized boxes of detergent. Supersized meals. Big-screen TVs. Vehicles with extra leg room, extra head room and vast storage space.

The bigger-is-better phenomenon affects the workplace too. Associates vie for the biggest office, the heftiest raise, the longest service record. About the only thing we want to be small is our lap-top computers – but even then we want them to have large memory capacity and a multitude of special features.

Our God is certainly capable of big feats. He parted the Red Sea. He created the universe in less than a week. But it's better not to measure our business success by how much money we earn. God isn't interested in the size of your salary. He's interested in your life and the small but faithful steps you take towards Him.

Remember, a little obedience and faithfulness makes a big difference to God.

Everything is funny as long as it is happening to somebody else.

There is a right time for everything . . . A time to laugh.

Ecclesiastes 3:1,4 TLB

A professional carpet layer stepped back to survey the new carpet he had just installed in a home. He was proud of his work and hungry from the effort. He reached into his jacket pocket for the chocolate bar he had been saving for break time and found his pocket empty. He looked across the home's vast living room. There, in the middle of his expertly laid carpet, he noticed a lump – a chocolate-bar-sized lump.

The carpet layer's heart sank as he realized that there was no way to retrieve his snack without tearing up his work and beginning again. He thought for a few moments, then grabbed his hammer and beat the lump flat, destroying any evidence of his embarrassing mistake.

Then he exited the home as if it were on fire.

As the man climbed into his truck a few moments later, he saw his chocolate bar lying on the seat. Puzzled, he unwrapped his treat and gobbled it down. Just as he was about to start his truck, the home-owner hurried out of his house, frantic. 'Excuse me,' he said to the carpet layer, 'but while you were laying the carpet, did you notice my son's gerbil? It seems to have escaped, and we can't find it anywhere!'

Difficulty in achieving your goals will reveal one of two things: what you are made of – or what you are full of.

Work hard so God can say to you, 'Well done.'

2 Timothy 2:15 TLB

Wayne Dyer wrote a book that he believed was important and much-needed by a lot of people.

Upon completing his book, he began to search for a publisher. All his search brought him were rejection slips. Not one publisher saw any market for Dyer's work.

Discouraged but undaunted, he dipped into his own pocket and published the book himself.

Then, he took to the roads to peddle it. He'd arrange appearances on local talk shows around the country, then stuff his car full of books and tell local booksellers he was going to be on the radio or TV the next day – and that he would provide them books to meet the demand created by his appearance. He did this for two years, selling a few books at a time.

One night he taped a show in San Francisco – at 3 a.m. About seventeen people were tuned in. But, one of the people was Johnny Carson. Carson loved Dyer's stuff. Soon, Dyer appeared on *The Tonight Show*, and sales of his book *Your Erroneous Zones* skyrocketed. Dyer became a best-selling author and didn't have to do any more 3 a.m. tapings.

The lesson here: Always do your best and never, never give up. You never know who may be listening, or watching, or reading.

The way a team plays as a whole determines its success. You may have the greatest bunch of individual stars in the world, but if they don't play together, the club won't be worth a dime.

Two can accomplish more than twice as much as one, for the results can be much better.
Ecclesiastes 4:9 TLB

The emperor penguins of Antarctica know the importance of teamwork. They huddle together by the thousands, providing enough warmth to survive the brutal, freezing weather~ which can make a hunk of steel as brittle as a potato chip.

The penguins take turns monitoring the outside of their giant huddle, on the lookout for danger or food. After one of the birds has finished 'perimeter duty', it moves to the inside of the group so it can get warm and sleep. The baby penguins stand on their mums' and dads' feet to protect themselves from the icy surfaces. If a penguin, big or small, tried to make it on its own, it wouldn't survive one frozen winter night.

We can all learn from penguins. Teamwork equals survival. And the tougher the conditions, the more important it is for workers to band together. You may not ever need to share physical warmth – unless the heater goes off – but you can share encouragement, empathy and ideas. You can share the work load in times of crisis – and you can share the credit when success is achieved.

Don't worry
about doing what
is profitable,
prudent, or
politically correct.
Do what's right.

*Act with courage, and may the
Lord be with those who do well.*

2 Chronicles 19:11

James Burke, CEO of Johnson & Johnson, was facing a crisis. Someone had tampered with a few bottles of his Tylenol pain relievers and Burke needed to respond to the public. He wanted to recall the product – remove it from the shelves completely until the source and scope of the tampering could be determined. His lawyers, financial advisors and high-priced business consultants advised him that such a move was unnecessary – not to mention difficult to undertake and brutally expensive.

Despite the pressure, Burke removed every bottle of Tylenol from shelves across the country. He said that putting himself in a customer's shoes led him to the right decision.

'If I'm a mother and use Tylenol,' he said, 'am I ever going to buy it again if there's the slightest chance of playing Russian roulette with my child's wellbeing?'

Today, Tylenol fills the shelves of supermarkets nationwide – featuring safety caps pioneered by Burke. People felt they could trust a man who was willing to sustain a great financial loss rather than jeopardize the safety of children. Burke survived a potential crisis by acting on the strength of his convictions, not the misguided, panicky opinions of others.

Our greatest glory
is not in never falling,
but in rising
every time we fall.

Encourage one another daily,
as long as it is called Today.
Hebrews 3:13

As a young boy in Naples, Italy, he toiled long hours in a factory. All the while, he dreamed of being a great singer. At the age of ten he took his first voice lesson. After hearing his voice, his teacher said bluntly, 'You can't sing. You haven't any voice at all. Your voice sounds like the wind in the shutters.' Not exactly the food a dream needs in order to grow.

The boy's mother, however, heard something else in her son's voice – potential greatness. She believed in him. Even though the family was poor, she assured her son, 'My boy, I am going to make every sacrifice to pay for your voice lessons.'

The mother's confidence and constant encouragement paid off. The boy became one of the most loved and critically acclaimed singers in the world: Enrico Caruso.

As an employee, what are your special talents, your dreams? What can you do to nurture your gifts – and the gifts of those who work with you? Do you know someone who is ready to give up on a dream? What can you do to help that person keep the dream alive?

The gifts God gives must be developed, so that the world can open these gifts and enjoy them.

An ounce of leading by example is worth a pound of pressure.

'I have set you an example that you should do as I have done for you.'

John 13:15

Ben Franklin wanted Philadelphia to lighten up. He believed that lighting the city's streets would not only improve it aesthetically, but also make it safer. But he didn't try to persuade Philly's citizens by talking to them. Instead, he hung a beautiful lantern near his front door. He kept the lantern brightly polished, and carefully and faithfully lit the wick each evening just before dusk.

People strolling the dark street saw Franklin's light from a long way off. They found its glow to be friendly and beautiful – and a helpful, guiding landmark. Soon, Franklin's neighbours began placing lanterns in front of their own homes. Before long, the whole city was dotted with light, and more and more people began to appreciate the beauty and value of Franklin's bright idea.

Lighting the streets became a city-wide – and city-sponsored – endeavour.

Just as Franklin became a point of light for his city, our actions can become beacons for our co-workers. What they see, they copy. And when they see the light, they may be inspired to illuminate a candle of their own.

Honesty
is the cornerstone
of all success.

Truthful lips endure forever.
Proverbs 12:19

The children of a prominent family wondered what to give their father as a gift. Finally, they decided to commission a professional biographer to write a book chronicling the family's history. The children met with the writer and provided many documents and anecdotes to weave into his story – along with dozens of photos.

One of the children pointed out, 'We have one more matter we need to discuss with you – our family's wayward sheep.' Then, in hushed tones, he told the biographer about an uncle who had been convicted of first-degree murder and executed in the electric chair.

'No problem,' the biographer assured the children. 'I can handle this information in a way that will avoid embarrassment.'

'We don't want to lie,' said one of the children.

'No problem,' the biographer repeated. "I'll just say that your Uncle Samuel occupied a chair of applied electronics at an important government institution. He was attached to his position by the strongest of ties, and his death came as a real shock.'

Think about your written and spoken communication at work. It can be technically accurate without being true. Pursue truth.

Humans are born with two eyes, but with one tongue, in order that they should see twice as much as they say.

Don't talk so much. You keep putting your foot in your mouth. Be sensible and turn off the flow!

Proverbs 10:19 TLB

A young executive, fresh out of business school, entered his office for his first day of work. Settling into his leather chair, he breathed a sigh of satisfaction and adjusted his silk Hermes tie. He had toiled long and hard to get where he was. He leaned back to savour the moment. Then, noticing a prospective client coming towards his office door, he began to look busy and energetic. He opened a notebook, then picked up his phone, cradling the receiver under his chin.

As the client entered the office, the neophyte executive began to write furiously, while stating in his most business-like tone, 'Very good, then, Mr Forsythe. I will meet with you on Friday to finalize the deal. What's that? Yes, four million should be adequate. I will notify the New York office of our agreement.'

Hanging up the phone, the executive put down his pen and extended his hand to his visitor.

'Good morning, sir,' he said in his most officious tone. 'How may I help you?'

The 'client' replied, 'Actually, I'm here to hook up your phone.'

Don't go out of your way to impress people-especially if it means putting on airs. Nothing makes a worse impression than someone falling on his or her face.

To hit the mark, we aim above the mark.

I can do all things through Him who strengthens me.

Philippians 4:13 NASB

A young businesswoman, confused about her future, sat in a park, watching squirrels scamper among the trees. Suddenly, a squirrel leapt from one high branch towards another quite a distance away. To the woman, the leap seemed suicidal. And, just as the woman feared, the squirrel missed the branch it was aiming for-but landed safely on a branch several feet below.

A man sitting on a nearby bench remarked, 'I've seen many squirrels miss their branches, but I've never seen any get hurt trying.' He chuckled and added, 'I guess they have to risk something if they don't want to spend their whole lives in the same old tree.'

The woman contemplated the man's words. *A squirrel takes its chances*, she thought, *do I have less nerve than a squirrel? Am I nuts?* At that moment, she made up her mind to take the career risk she had been considering. Later, she landed safely, ultimately climbing to a higher position than she had even dared to imagine.

What are your career dreams? Do they seem out of reach? Don't be afraid to take a leap of faith now and then. If you miss, God will catch you.

An investment in knowledge always pays the best interest.

Do you see a man skilled in his work? He will serve before kings; he will not serve before obscure men.

Proverbs 22:29

Alexander Graham Bell spent five frustrating, financially draining years experimenting with a variety of materials in the hope of making a metal disk that, vibrating in response to sound, could reproduce those sounds and send them over an electrified wire.

During a visit to Washington, DC, Bell called on Joseph Henry, a scientist who was a pioneer in electronics. Bell presented his ideas to Henry and asked his advice. He wondered if he should pursue his 'telephone' idea – given that he lacked the necessary knowledge of electricity. Henry's advice was simple: 'If you don't have the know-how, get it.'

So, with a steadfast fervour, Bell studied electricity. A year later, when he earned a patent for the telephone, patent-office officials credited him for knowing more about electricity than all the other inventors of his day combined.

Diligence. Studiousness. Hard work. Hope. Perseverance. They are common words. These words are the keys, however, to gaining the skills to do anything uncommonly well.

I have yet to find the person, however exalted in his or her station, who did not do better work and put forth greater effort under a spirit of approval than under a spirit of criticism.

Be patient with each other,
making allowance for each other's
faults because of your love.
Ephesians 4:2 TLB

A group of parents watched from the stands as their local school's marching band performed on the field. The band was doing well, executing its formations with perfect precision. Almost.

One band member, a trumpet player, was noticeably out of synch. He veered right when his band-mates veered left. He was always a second late getting his instrument to his mouth.

And when he marched along, he placed down his right foot when everyone else was landing on the left foot.

From the stands, the trumpeter's mother looked on. With exultant pride, she turned to her husband and exclaimed, 'Will you look at that? The whole band is out of step – except for Jimmy!'

Unlike this mother, we can't always gloss over our co-workers' mistakes and weaknesses. But addressing such issues gently, tactfully and privately is the best way to help others improve their work and become stronger, more confident workers. We can choose to care about those around us in spite of their mistakes. And we can choose, too, to focus on the traits that make our colleagues special, valuable and likeable.

An employee is fed with pay cheques – and praise.

Do not let any unwholesome talk come out of your mouths, but only what is helpful for building others up according to their needs, that it may benefit those who listen.

Ephesians 4:29

If you are a boss or hope to be one someday, consider these suggestions for managers, written from an employee's viewpoint:

- My mind doesn't hold the same information, the same experience, that yours does. As you instruct me, please go slowly so that I can keep up with you.
- My eyes have not seen the business world as yours have. Let me explore some of it on my own. Please don't restrict me unnecessarily.
- This company will probably be around for years and years. But I may be here for only a portion of that time. Let's take the time to get to know each other and make the most of the time we work together.
- My feelings are tender. Don't speak harshly to me or embarrass me in front of my colleagues. Don't chastise me for being inquisitive.
- I am a child of God; please treat me as such. Value my talents and uniqueness.
- To grow as an employee, I need your encouragement. If you tell me what I do right, I can repeat successes. And when you must reprimand, please remember that you can criticize my work without criticizing me as a person.

Work should be a place where leaders serve and servers lead.

'Many that are first shall be last; and the last shall be first.'

Matthew 19:30 KJV

Two pure-bred French poodles strolled through a park, their ebony noses high in the air.

Rounding a corner, they encountered a scruffy mutt with a bad case of mange – and a worse case of halitosis. They tried to sidestep this common alley hound, but it was eager to make friends and trotted along beside them, barking happily.

'Excuse us, please,' one of the poodles yapped icily, 'we have things we must attend to.'

'All right,' the mutt replied, 'but at least tell me your names, so I know what to call you if our paths cross again.'

'If you must know,' the poodle answered, 'my name is Yvette, spelled Y-V-E-T-T-E, and my colleague here is Charlemagne, spelled C-H-A-R-L-E-M-A-G-N-E.'

'Pleased to meet you!' the mutt said. Then, imitating the poodle's tone, it noted, 'My name is Fido-P-H-Y-D-E-A-U-X. Now, if you'll excuse me, I have some garbage to roll in.'

The job is no place for prideful poodles. Respect and dignity, yes. But haughty arrogance born of position and bloodline? That is barking up the wrong tree. Ultimately, the workplace should be marked by equal-opportunity caring – a place where every dog can have its day.

The world's best face-lift is a smile.

There is a time for everything . . . a time to laugh.

Ecclesiastes 3:1,4

A restaurant famous for its freshly-squeezed lemon juice had a standing offer to its patrons. The restaurant employed a huge assistant cook, Lars, who often squeezed juice out of lemons with massive, callused hands. The restaurant offered $100 to anyone who could coax just one drop from a lemon after Lars was done with it.

For years, customers took the lemon test – and failed. Then, one spring day, a tiny bespectacled man entered the restaurant. In a high-pitched voice, he announced, 'I'm here to win the hundred bucks.'

Lars grabbed a lemon in his meaty right paw and bled the juice from it. With a grunt, he gave the lemon one last squeeze before handing it to the diminutive customer.

The man held the lemon in his dainty hand and began to squeeze. For a few moments, nothing happened. But then, one drop emerged from the rind of the lemon and tumbled to the countertop. As the man smiled, another drop fell, then another and another. Soon, a small puddle of lemon juice had formed on the counter.

'You're amazing!' Lars told the man as he handed him a crisp $100 bill. 'Are you some kind of martial-arts expert? A professional wrestler?'

'None of the above,' said the customer, still smiling. 'I work for the tax department.'

The person you truly are is the person who emerges when no one is looking.

Serve wholeheartedly, as if you were serving the Lord, not men, because you know that the Lord will reward everyone for whatever good he does.

Ephesians 6:7

Marty Logan was a skilled and loyal carpenter who worked almost two decades for a successful contractor. One day, the contractor called Marty into his office and said, 'I'm putting you in charge of the next house we build. I want you to order all the materials and oversee the job from the ground up.'

Marty accepted the assignment enthusiastically. He studied the blueprints and double-checked every measurement and specification. As he worked, a thought crept into his mind: *Hey, I'm in charge here, so I can cut a few corners if I want to. I can use less-expensive materials, subcontract cheaper labour, then pocket the extra money. Who will ever know? I've worked hard for almost twenty years. I deserve a little 'bonus'.*

So, Marty ordered second-grade lumber and inexpensive concrete. He put in cheap wiring and hired unskilled minimum-wage workers. When the home was finished, the contractor came to give it a quick once-over.

'Looks like a fine job, as usual, Marty,' he said. 'And now I have a surprise for you. You've been such a faithful carpenter for me all these years that I've decided to give you this house as a reward!'

Build well today. Directly or indirectly, you will have to live with the character and reputation you construct.

Every job is a self-portrait
of the one who does it.
Is your work a masterpiece
or a hack-job?

*Whatever you do, work at it
with all your heart, as working
for the Lord, not for men.*
Colossians 3:23

Long ago, a band of minstrels tried to make a living by travelling from village to village, performing music. However, even though the band's fee was small, the common folk to whom their music appealed could not afford admission to their performances.

Discouraged, one of the musicians said, 'I see no reason to perform tonight. It's snowing, and no one will come out on an evening like this.'

One of the others agreed. 'He's right. Only a handful of people came last night.'

However, the leader of the troupe disagreed: 'I know you're discouraged. I am too. But we have a responsibility to those who might come tonight. We will give our best performance. It's not the fault of those who come that others do not.'

Heartened by their leader's words, the minstrels played to their sparse crowd with passion and energy. After the show, the leader again addressed the troupe. In his hand he held a note handed to him by one of the few audience members. The leader read the note: 'Thank you for the beautiful performance.' It was signed simply, 'Your King'.

Everything that you do is performed before your King – the King of Kings. Are your words and deeds worthy of His audience?

The world's best business and personal Consultant is always just a prayer away.

Devote yourselves to prayer, keeping alert in it with thanksgiving.

Colossians 4:2 NRSV

When Dwight D. Eisenhower led the Allied invasion of Europe during World War II, he faced the responsibility of making one of the most difficult and far-reaching decisions ever tackled by a single person. He made the decision to change the date of the D-Day invasion at the last moment. The potential consequences were so overwhelming that Ike felt almost crushed by their weight. Still, he was the Supreme Commander and the only one trusted to make a choice that would impact the lives of millions.

Writing about the pressure, Eisenhower noted, 'I knew I did not have the required wisdom. But I turned to God. I asked God to give me the wisdom. I yielded myself to Him. I surrendered myself. And He gave me clear guidance. He gave me insight to see what was right, and He endowed me with courage to make my decision. And finally, He gave me peace of mind in the knowledge that, having been guided by God to the decision, I could leave the results to Him.'

The decisions you make in your job might not approach the magnitude of General Eisenhower's. But whatever the size of the problem, God wants you to trust Him and let Him guide you through it.

The difference between genius and stupidity is that genius has its limits.

For we are God's workmanship, created in Christ Jesus to do good works, which God prepared in advance for us to do.

Ephesians 2:10

A partially deaf boy trudged home one day from school. In his hand, he carried a note. It was a note from school officials, suggesting that his parents remove him from school. According to those wise officials, this boy was 'too stupid to learn'.

Upon reading the note, the boy's mother vowed, 'My son Tom isn't too stupid to learn. I'll teach him myself.' And that is exactly what she did.

Many years later when Tom died, many Americans paid tribute to him by turning off their lights for one full minute. This was a fitting tribute, for Tom Edison invented the light bulb – along with motion pictures and the phonograph. In all, he was credited with more than a thousand patents. He also had a gift for powerful, motivating words. You will read several of his quotes in this book.

Neither you nor anyone you work with is beyond learning. No one is beyond discovering new ways to express talent, enthusiasm, creativity and love. No one is beyond receiving affection and encouragement.

Never give up on yourself, no matter what anyone else says. Stand up for others and encourage them to stay the course as well. Your Heavenly Father hasn't given up on any of you. And He never will.

The best way to make workers miserable is to satisfy all of their demands.

Be content with what you have.
Hebrews 13:5

In *Little Women*, Mrs March tells this story to her daughters: Once upon a time, there were four girls who had enough to eat and drink and wear, a good many comforts and pleasures, kind friends and parents – and yet they were not content, always wishing for something more.

Finally they asked an old woman for advice. 'When you feel discontented,' she told them, 'think over your blessings, and be grateful.'

They decided to try her advice and were surprised to see how well off they were. One girl discovered money couldn't keep shame and sorrow out of rich people's houses. Another learned she was a great deal happier with her youth, health and good spirits than a certain fretful, feeble old lady who couldn't enjoy her comforts. The third found that, disagreeable as it was to help get dinner, it was harder still to have to go begging for it. The fourth girl learned that even carnelian rings were not so valuable as good behaviour. So they agreed to stop complaining and to enjoy the blessings they already possessed.

Wanting something does not mean it's best for us. If you want to be content, learn to be grateful for what you have.

A good example
is the best sermon.

Whatever you have learned or received or heard from me, or seen in me – put it into practice. And the God of peace will be with you.

Philippians 4:9

Four men stood in a church lobby. They were arguing over which Bible translation was the best. One argued for the King James Version, citing its beautiful, eloquent old English.

The second man advocated the New International Version, noting its literalism and the confidence he felt in its commitment to accurately representing the message of the original texts. The third man praised *The Living Bible* for its conversational, easy-to-understand prose.

After giving thought to each of his friends' impassioned arguments, the fourth man said with certainty, 'Frankly, I prefer my boss's translation.'

'What do you mean?' the first man asked incredulously. 'Your boss is just a shop foreman. He doesn't even have a college degree.'

"I stand by my claim,' the fourth man said. 'My boss has translated the pages of the Bible into his life. He has lived the message. And it has been the most convincing translation I have ever witnessed.'

All the scholarly theological pursuits can't match the life lived through love and marked by kindness, truthfulness and humility. That, in fact, is the way of living that is taught in every translation of the Scriptures.

That day is lost
in which one
has not laughed.

Our mouths were filled with laughter.

Psalm 126:2

Here's a poem entitled 'Just Another Day at the Office'. See if you can relate to it.

My assistant is out sick today.
The printer's out of toner.
My car is in the shop again,
So I'm forced to drive a loaner.
Two new software programs to learn,
But the verbiage makes me dizzy.
I've tried to call up tech support,
But their line is always busy.
The repairman's torn the copier apart,
So my report will be quite late.
With people swooping in like flies,
How can I concentrate?
The telephone rings endlessly.
There's gossip in the hall.
My candy dish is empty now.
And a salesman's come to call.
Sometimes I'd like to chuck it all.
Trade this madness in for boredom.
But the kids need braces, clothes, and shoes,
And how else can I afford them?

The greatest good
you can do for
others is, not just to
share your riches,
but to reveal to them
their own.

Honour one another above yourselves.
Romans 12:10

In the 1800s two powerful men vied for leadership of Britain's government: William Gladstone and Benjamin Disraeli. They were intense rivals. Disraeli once said of his opponent, 'The difference between a misfortune and a calamity [is this]: If Gladstone fell into the Thames, it would be a misfortune. But if someone dragged him out again, it would be a calamity.'

Both men proved to be successful leaders, but Disraeli was seen as a man of more charisma – and that edge was due to something other than his razor-sharp wit. The key to Disraeli's charismatic edge was best expressed by a woman who dined with the two statesmen on consecutive evenings.

When asked about her impressions of them, she said, 'When I left the dining room after sitting next to Mr Gladstone, I thought he was the cleverest man in England. But after sitting next to Mr Disraeli, I thought I was the cleverest woman in England.'

The key to being an inspiring leader is not trying to prove how important and smart you are. As Disraeli knew, the true secret lies in one's ability to make others feel important and valued.

Nothing great in the world has been accomplished without passion.

All hard work brings a profit, but mere talk leads only to poverty.

Proverbs 14:23

The famed artist Michelangelo was summoned to Rome by Pope Julius II to work on a painting project. Michelangelo wanted to refuse the task, which involved painting a dozen figures on the ceiling of a small chapel in the Vatican. Michelangelo was a trained painter, but his true passion was sculpture. However, when pressed, Michelangelo reluctantly accepted the task.

The artist's rivals hoped he would fail in his assignment, knowing that painting was not his first love. But once Michelangelo agreed to do the job, he poured himself into it. He expanded the scope of the project from a simple depiction of the twelve apostles to include more than 400 figures and nine scenes from the book of Genesis.

For four agonizing years, Michelangelo lay on his back painting the Sistine Chapel's ceiling. His neck, shoulders and back ached. Paint dripped into his eyes. His vision was damaged. Later, Michelangelo would call this time 'tortured years' that made him feel 'as old and as weary as Jeremiah'.

However, the fruits of this agony were beautiful. Art historians note that artists like Raphael adapted their styles to reflect Michelangelo's influence. What drove Michelangelo's commitment to excellence and beauty? 'No one will ever see this corner of the chapel,' someone called up to him as he worked one day.

His reply was simple: 'God will see.'

To give anything less than your best is to sacrifice the gift.

A wise man will hear, and will increase learning.

Proverbs 1:5 KJV

You never know where or how you will hear words that will change your life. A fifteen-year-old basketball player was attending a summer basketball camp run by a man named Easy Ed Macauley. At one point, Macauley told his young hoopsters, 'Just remember that if you're not working at your game to the utmost of your ability, there will be someone out there somewhere with equal ability who is doing the work. And one day you'll play each other, and he'll have the advantage.'

Those words profoundly affected at least one player – young Bill Bradley. Bradley lived those words. He worked hard on his game and became an excellent high-school hoopster, then star college player at Princeton. Still driven, he elevated his talents to yet another level and became a key member of the great New York Knicks' teams.

Even that wasn't enough for Bradley. After retiring from basketball, he entered politics and ran for the office of President of the United States.

What are you doing to 'work on your game' in all aspects of your life? What are you doing to distinguish yourself from the others who practise the same craft that you do? If you were to compete against them, who would have the advantage?

Getting off your bottom is the first step in getting to the top.

The sluggard's craving will be the death of him, because his hands refuse to work.
Proverbs 21:25

One autumn day in 1894, Guglielmo entered his room on the third floor of his parents' home.

He had spent the entire summer reading books and filling notebooks with squiggly diagrams.

Now he continued his vigil, rising early and working long into the night. His mother became alarmed as his frame became thinner, his face drawn, his eyes weary.

But, one day, he announced that his work was complete. He invited the family to his third-floor room. He pushed a button. On the first floor, a bell rang-a bell not connected to the button by wires! His mother was amazed. But not his father. He saw no use in being able to send a signal such a short distance.

Guglielmo went back to work. He relayed a signal from one hill to the next. Then to an area beyond the hill. Eventually, his invention was perfected.

Guglielmo Marconi was ultimately hailed as the inventor of wireless telegraphy – the forerunner of the radio. Marconi received a Nobel prize in physics for his effort – and a seat in the Italian senate.

Vision and effort do pay off. Remember that as you work towards your goals. And if you'd like to listen to the radio while you work, Guglielmo Marconi probably wouldn't mind a bit.

Our greatest danger in life is in permitting the urgent things to crowd out the important.

'Where your treasure is, there your heart will be also.'

Matthew 6:21

A time-management expert addressed a group of business students. He pulled out a one-gallon Mason jar and set it on the table. Then he produced a dozen fist-sized rocks and carefully placed them into the jar. Then he asked, 'Is this jar full?'

Everyone said yes. Then he reached under the table and pulled out a bucket of gravel. He dumped it in and shook the jar. He asked the group again, 'Is the jar full?'

By this time the class was on to him. 'Probably not,' one student answered. Then the instructor reached under the table and grabbed a bucket of sand. He poured in the sand, which went into all of the spaces between the rocks and the gravel. He asked, 'Is this jar full?'

'No!' the class shouted.

Next, he grabbed a jug of water and began to pour it in until the jar was filled to the brim.

'What is the point of this illustration?' he asked.

One student offered, 'No matter how full your schedule is, you can always fit some more things in it!'

'No,' the speaker replied, 'the truth this illustration teaches us is: if you don't put the big rocks in first, you'll never get them in.'

Ask yourself, 'What are the "big rocks" in my life?' Put those in your jar first.

Brevity is
the soul
of wit.

When words are many, sin is not absent,
but he who holds his tongue is wise.
Proverbs 10:19

Some people believe that important messages and decisions must be conveyed with much verbiage and fanfare. The humble and wise President Abraham Lincoln wasn't one of those people. On April 7, 1865, with the Civil War raging, Lincoln needed to communicate with one of his generals on the front lines. His credibility as president – and the country's future – hung in the balance. He wanted his message to inspire, but also to be clear. Here's what he wrote:

> Lieut. Gen. Grant,
> Gen. Sheridan says, 'If the thing is pressed, I think Lee will surrender.' Let the thing be pressed.
> Lincoln

Lincoln was a brilliant, effective communicator. He knew that few things are as effective as simplicity and directness. His famous Gettysburg Address is another example of succinct communication. Too many words can take up more of one's time than is necessary and often serve the deliverer of the message rather than the receiver. What's more, lengthy messages can become confusing and diluted, losing the original intent altogether.

As you communicate at work and in life, follow Lincoln's example. There's no need to complicate your message with needless jargon or equivocation. Say what you mean. Then send that e-mail, issue that memo, or end that phone call. Keep it short and simple.

Courage is fear that has said its prayers.

Be strong and courageous.

Deuteronomy 31:6

A racing driver who set the world speed record. A fighter pilot who recorded the most aerial-combat victories against the Germans in World War I. A man who survived a plane crash and spent twenty-two days on a raft in the Pacific Ocean. What do these three have in common?

They are all the same person: Eddie Rickenbacker. When Eddie was twelve, his father died. So Eddie left school to become the family breadwinner, doing whatever he had to do to help the family survive.

As a teenager, he started working as a racing car mechanic. By the time he was twenty-two, he, himself, was racing. Two years later, he set the world speed record at Daytona.

When World War I began, Eddie tried to enlist as an aviator but was told he was over-aged and under-educated. He eventually talked his superiors into sending him to flight training.

By the war's end, he had logged 300 combat hours and survived 134 aerial encounters, shooting down twenty-six enemy planes.

When asked the secret to his success, Rickenbacker cited courage. 'Courage,' he told them, 'is doing what you're afraid to do. There can be no courage unless you're scared.'

Fear is natural. It can overcome you, or you can say, as Eddie Rickenbacker did a thousand times, 'I'll fight like a wildcat!'

I skate where the puck is going to be, not where it has been.

Be very careful, then, how you live–not as unwise but as wise, making the most of every opportunity.

Ephesians 5:15–16

For years, the Swiss were the kings of watch-making. They built the best timepieces money could buy. By the 1940s, they produced 80 per cent of the world's watches.

But in the late 1960s, an inventor approached a leading Swiss watch company with an idea for a new kind of watch. This firm rejected the inventor's idea, as did every other Swiss company he courted.

Still believing his design had merit, the man took it to Japan. And a company there was intrigued by the invention – a digital watch. The name of the company was Seiko. Seiko began producing digital watches, which today constitute 80 pe cent of all watches produced – the same percentage once claimed by the Swiss.

Today's market leaders may not be tomorrow's. Only those who have the foresight to anticipate the future and improve their products and/or services can compete in today's rapidly changing, innovation-driven society. Even if you have a sizeable lead on your competitors, you will eventually get passed if you stop moving forward.

For companies – or individuals – to thrive, it is imperative to embrace new ideas and different ways of doing things. When it comes to new ideas, keep an open mind.

Luck is what happens when preparation meets opportunity.

Whatsoever a man soweth, that shall he also reap.

Galatians 6:7 KJV

If you met Tony Gwynn on the street, you might not guess he is a professional athlete. At 5'11" and 220 pounds, he's a bit on the chubby side. But if you watched him play baseball, you'd have no doubt about his athletic prowess. For many years, he has been baseball's most consistent hitter. He has eight batting titles to his credit – if not for injuries, he'd have more.

What makes Gwynn such as exceptional hitter? Focus and dedication. Several times each season, Gwynn devours Ted Williams's book, *The Science of Hitting*, a book he's been reading since college. And he watches countless hours of videos on hitting. He also loves to talk hitting with his peers, and he's been known to arrive at social events with a batting glove hanging from his pocket.

And when he's not playing, talking or watching baseball, you might find Gwynn playing Ping-Pong or some other activity that will increase his hand–eye coordination.

You may feel that you lack some of the natural physical or intellectual tools to excel at your vocation. But if you are willing to focus on the details that lead to excellence, you could be a big hit in your chosen field!

There's a name for people who aren't passionate about their work: unemployed.

He who walks with the wise grows wise.

Proverbs 13:20

One day, Lester Wunderman was fired from his job with a New York advertising firm. Wunderman was discouraged and hurt, particularly because he knew that he could learn a lot from the agency's leader, Max Sackheim. So the next morning, Wunderman returned to his office and worked just as he had been doing – but without pay.

Sackheim ignored the young ex-employee for a month or so. Then, he finally relented. He approached Wunderman one day and said, 'OK, you win. I never saw a man who wanted a job more than he wanted money.'

Wunderman made the most of his second chance. He continued to learn from Sackheim and eventually went on to become one of the country's most successful ad executives. Some credit him with being the father of direct marketing.

What kind of initiative and boldness are you willing to take to gain the attention and confidence of your boss. How badly do you want to learn? And do you want a vocation – or a passion? Sometimes approaching what seems like ordinary work with extraordinary intent can produce unbelievable results.

The great pleasure in life is doing what people say you cannot do.

The LORD *will guide you always;*
he will satisfy your needs.
Isaiah 58:11

Gene was a great amateur boxer. He possessed great knockout power in both hands and was destined to become a top professional pugilist. But before turning pro, he broke both his hands. He would never be able to punch with the power he once possessed. Both his doctor and his manager told him he would never become a world champion.

Gene Tunney didn't listen to them. He believed he could excel at his profession, despite the major obstacle he encountered. 'If I can't become a champion as a [power] puncher,' he said, 'I'll make it as a boxer.'

So Tunney, knowing that he could no longer rely on his knockout power, set out to perfect his boxing skills. He learned to bob and weave and throw accurate – albeit less potent – punches.

In one of the biggest fights of his career, Tunney faced Jack Dempsey, known as the Manassa Mauler, a man with feared knockout power. But, using the skills he might not have developed if not for the injury, Tunney outboxed Dempsey and became the heavyweight champion of the world.

Life might alter the path you take to success, just as it did for Gene Tunney. But that doesn't mean you can't still get to where you want to go.

Experience is not
what happens to a person,
it is what a person does
with what happens to
him or her.

*Let the wise listen and add to
their learning.*
Proverbs 1:5

Steve Martin knew he wanted to be an entertainer. He worked hard on a magic act, which he then began to try out on audiences. However, some of the tricks invariably went wrong.

Martin could have become discouraged, but he listened to and watched his audiences carefully. He noticed that the crowds would erupt with laughter when a trick went south.

In response to the audiences, Martin said, 'I went through my act and started taking out all the things that went right.'

Martin, in other words, performed the ultimate magic trick. He turned his illusionist act into a comedy routine and became the country's top stand-up act. And he's gone on to become a successful comic actor, director and writer.

Often, we are so focused on accomplishing a series of tasks, we don't take time to weigh the effectiveness – or necessity – of what we are doing. If we fail, we often take that as a signal to give up entirely. What do your clients and your co-workers really want? What do they respond to most enthusiastically and appreciatively? Is that what you are striving to give them, or are you futilely trying to pull a non-existent rabbit out of a hat?

God can do great things through people who don't care who gets the credit.

Be completely humble and gentle.

Ephesians 4:2

One night in 1837, a young woman named Florence believed she heard God's voice informing her that she had a mission. Nine years later, that mission began to take shape when a friend sent her information about the Institution of Protestant Deaconesses in Germany. She entered the Institution to learn how to care for the sick.

In 1853, Florence became superintendent of a woman's hospital in London. When the Crimean War broke out the following year, she volunteered at once to care for British soldiers, leaving for Constantinople in haste. Once there, she was given charge of nursing at a military hospital. Even though the doctors were hostile towards her and the hospital was deplorably filthy, she dug in her heels and began to care for her patients as best she could.

First she used provisions she had brought with her from London. Then she spearheaded a correspondence campaign to resupply the hospital. She spent many hours each day in the wards, caring for the soldiers who entered the hospital. The comfort she gave on night rounds earned her the nickname 'The Lady with the Lamp'.

This woman's selfless giving eventually made her name synonymous with compassionate nursing care. She was Florence Nightingale.

Some people would rather endure an enema than love an enemy.

'Love your enemies, do good to them, and lend to them without expecting to get anything back. Then your reward will be great.'

Luke 6:35

Is there any tougher commandment than the one that instructs us to love our enemies? Not tolerate them or simply do kind things for them. Love them. Those obnoxious, cruel, hateful people. The boss who treats you unfairly. The co-worker who pretends to be your friend, then back-stabs you. The unhappy customer who unfairly criticizes you and reports you to your superiors. The technical support person who is consistently rude. Or that certain someone who is simply annoying.

The first step in loving our enemies is praying for them (not for their humiliation, downfall or destruction, by the way). And when we pray for our enemies, we need to pray as much for our own attitudes and behaviour as for theirs. That way, even if our prayers don't change our enemies' ugly qualities, they will change us.

Often the first thing to pray for is simply the will and grace to *want* to love our enemies.

In praying for these people, we may come to realize that they are no less attractive to God, or loved by God, than we are. And as we experience what hard work it is to love unloveable people, we will value God's love for us more than ever.

One person with courage makes a majority.

The LORD detests lying lips, but he delights in men who are truthful.
Proverbs 12:22

A nineteenth-century preacher named Peter Cartwright was preparing his sermon one Sunday when he was warned that US President Andrew Jackson would be in the congregation. He was told to keep his remarks benign, so as not to offend the president.

During his message, Cartwright acknowledged his famous guest. 'I have been told that Andrew Jackson is in the congregation,' he said. 'And I have been asked to guard my remarks. What I must say is that Andrew Jackson will go to hell if he doesn't repent of his sin.'

Some people in the audience cringed. Others gasped. What would become of this outspoken pastor? What penalty might he face?

After the service, Jackson strode up to Cartwright. The noble preacher stood his ground.

'Sir,' the president said, 'if I had a regiment of men like you, I could whip the world.'

It's not always easy to speak the truth, especially if you're intimidated by the size or import of your audience. It's much easier to say what we believe people – especially our superiors – will want to hear. When you don't say what you truly believe, not only are you speaking untruthfully to others, but you are betraying your own ideas and convictions.

Speak what you believe – the results of such honesty might just surprise you.

If you fail
to plan,
you plan
to fail.

'Suppose one of you wants to build a tower. Will he not first sit down and estimate the cost to see if he has enough money to complete it?'
Luke 14:28

The owners of a Mexican restaurant in California thought they had devised a clever promotion. They began offering free lunch for life to anyone who would get a tattoo of the restaurant's logo – a red-sombrero-clad fellow riding a jet-powered ear of corn. The manager reasoned, 'What sane person would want Jimmy the Corn Man permanently inked into his or her-skin?'

In the weeks that followed, forty-plus people were sporting Jimmy on various parts of their anatomy. In a panic, the manager did some quick maths, calculating that just to feed those already emblazoned with Jimmy would cost the restaurant $5.8 million over the course of the next fifty years. With a face as red as Jimmy's sombrero, the manager halted the promotion at fifty people.

The California eatery could have learned a lesson from The Big Texan Steak Ranch in Amarillo, Texas. This establishment offers a free 72-ounce steak dinner to any patron who can wolf down the steak – plus a salad, shrimp cocktail, potato and roll – in an hour or less.

While a few people have accomplished this feat, most fail and have to pay $54.13 for their meals. On average, only one person in eight succeeds. That means for every one meal it gives away, The Big Texan racks up $378.91.

A good laugh is sunshine in a heart.

A happy heart is good medicine and a cheerful mind works healing.

Proverbs 17:22 AMP

People have to miss work occasionally for a variety of reasons. However, some of the reasons are more intriguing than others. Consider, if you will, these actual 'excuses' gleaned from phone messages, memos and e-mails:

- Please excuse me for missing work today. I forgot to get the Sunday paper off the porch, and when I found it on Monday, I thought it was Sunday.
- Please excuse me for missing work today. I was ill and had to go get shot.
- I am calling to inform you that I will be absent from work. I have to go get three teeth taken out of my face.
- Hi, this is Robert. Please excuse me from work on January 28, 29, 30, 31, and 32. Also 33.
- I will not be coming into the office tomorrow. I am being bothered by very close veins.
- This is Mary, calling to notify you that I won't be at work on Monday because I am very tired. I spent the weekend with the Marines.

Laughter is the joyous universal evergreen of life.

A glad heart makes a cheerful countenance.

Proverbs 15:13 AMP

Workplace Signs of the Times
(actual signs from businesses around the world):

- In a London department store: 'Bargain Basement Upstairs.'
- Outside a farm supplies store: 'Horse manure: 50 cents pre-packed bag, 20 cents – do it yourself.'
- Outside a second-hand shop: 'We exchange anything – bicycles, washing machines, etc. Why not bring your wife along and get a wonderful bargain?'
- Outside a town hall in the UK: 'The town hall is closed until opening. It will remain closed after being opened. Open tomorrow.'
- On a disco marquee: 'Smarts is the most exclusive disco in town. Everyone is welcome!'
- Notice in a dry cleaner's window: 'Anyone leaving their garments here for more than thirty days will be disposed of!'
- Notice in a health-food shop window: 'Closed due to illness.'
- On a repair shop door: 'We can repair anything. (Please knock hard – the bell doesn't work.)'
- Note in a mens' room in London office building: 'Toilet out of order. Please use floor below.'

If you were to put up a sign at the entry of your office or work area, what would it say? If you had only a few words, how would you word your professional or personal mission statement?

Abilities are like tax deductions – we either use them, or we lose them.

Do not neglect your gift.

1 Timothy 4:14

Imagine receiving a gift from a wealthy person who is renowned for his taste in selecting perfect and valuable presents for everyone on his list. Wouldn't this be a gift you would be eager to open?

Sadly, many people have been given gifts from the perfect Giver, but they never bother to open them or use them for their intended purpose.

God has given each of us abilities. And He never makes a mistake. His gifts are never the wrong size or style or inappropriate in any way. No one has ever needed to return a gift from God. If we open these heaven-sent gifts, we can then use them in a way that will benefit others and bring glory to our Creator. Do you know what your true gifts are? Are you using them? Or are they lying dormant, gathering dust? If so, it's time to tear into that aging wrapping paper.

Putting your God-given talents to work is one of the most satisfying things you can do. As you do what God created you for, you gain a deep sense of purpose and become closer and more grateful to the One who gave you your talents. Few things are as beautiful as Creator and creation working together. Do what you can with what you've been given.

Envy takes the joy, happiness, and contentment out of living.

Keep your lives free from the love of money and be content with what you have.

Hebrews 13:5

Jealousy isn't referred to as the 'big green-eyed monster' for nothing. God hates jealousy so much that it made His top-ten list – the Ten Commandments. He etched in stone the following words: 'You shall not covet your neighbour's wife, or his manservant or maidservant, his ox, or donkey, or anything that belongs to your neighbour.'

In workplace terms, this commandment from the book of Exodus could read, 'You shall not covet your co-worker's salary, his corner office or award plaques, his title, budget or privileges, or his favoured status with the managing director.'

We are all God's children, and we shouldn't compare our 'blessings' with those of others.

When we envy what others have, we rob ourselves of the joy and contentment we should find in what God gives us. The emotion of jealousy is so powerful that it overtakes and squelches the positive energy we could be using to better ourselves – in the office and in our personal lives.

Guard your heart. If you find yourself unable to rejoice in the success of others, beware.

And instead of focusing on what others have, ask God to remind you of the many blessings, gifts and talents He has given you – and how many of them are undeserved.

Anxiety is the misuse of the imagination.

May the Lord of peace himself give you peace at all times and in every way.

2 Thessalonians 3:16

The Apostle Paul instructed believers to 'be anxious for nothing'. Think about that. Paul says the child of God shouldn't worry about anything! And Paul didn't give this advice lightly. He was in prison at the time he wrote it. In fact, he spent a lot of time in chains at various 'grey-bar hotels' – separated from those he loved. He had his well-publicized 'thorn in the flesh' to contend with as well.

Paul was a man who endured beatings and stonings. He even had disagreements with one of Jesus' original disciples, Peter. Ultimately, his staunch faith in God and his outspokenness about it got him beheaded.

Despite all his trials, Paul knew God could bring peace. God doesn't always untie all the knots in our lives. But He does give us the grace to live with the knots. So remember, there is nothing you face that is too difficult, too troubling or too frightening for God.

Follow Paul's example: He put it this way: 'The Lord is near. Do not be anxious about anything, but in everything, by prayer and petition, with thanksgiving, present your requests to God. And the peace of God, which transcends all understanding, will guard your hearts and your minds in Christ Jesus' (Philippians 4:5–7).

That feeling – the finish line, the last couple of meters – is what motivates me. If I could bottle that up and sell it, I'd be the richest man in the world.

He gives power to the tired and worn out, and strength to the weak.
Isaiah 40:29 TLB

After winning the gruelling Tour de France in 1999, cyclist Lance Armstrong went on to repeat the feat in the year 2000. Armstrong won both these races and a score of others after battling cancer, a cancer so devastating that it had spread throughout his body, even to his brain.

After his remarkable victory in the 1999 Tour de France, Armstrong said that he wouldn't have been able to win if not for the cancer! The drive, the perseverance and the courage that he developed while battling his internal enemy made him strong enough to ride faster and harder – and with more determination – than all of his opponents.

When athletes like Armstrong train, they run, ride or lift weights to the point of muscle failure. Although this approach actually breaks down muscle fibres, it is beneficial because the body adapts to the stress and rebuilds the damaged fibres to be stronger than ever.

Certainly, the pain and trials that confront us come from many different sources. But it could be that God allows them simply to make us stronger and better able to overcome our frailties and become all He intended us to be. Lance Armstrong knew the truth of the American proverb: 'In the presence of trials, some buy crutches. But others grow wings.'

Your companions are
like buttons
on an elevator.
They will either
take you up or
take you down.

He who walks with the wise grows wise,
but a companion of fools suffers harm.
Proverbs 13:20

Companionship choices are difficult to make. Jesus spent time with many people of low reputation, even to the point of being accused of being a low-life Himself. Yet we are cautioned in Proverbs that 'bad company corrupts good character'. The key to following Jesus' example and protecting ourselves lies in discernment.

First, we should spend as much time as possible with godly people who will encourage us to grow closer to our Creator. Second, as we befriend troubled people, we must be careful to do so on our terms, as much as possible. Certainly, in our job we don't have total control of whom we hang around with. But we do have to exercise control over the setting. It's unwise to join in or stand silently by while a group of associates gossips maliciously about someone else in the company.

And it's foolish to be around when associates are illegally using company equipment or resources (e.g., viewing pornography on the Internet or gambling with expense money).

At work we are known largely by the company we keep. There's nothing wrong with trying to be a positive influence among people who need a good role model. But when swimming with the sharks, we must constantly ask ourselves, 'Am I drawing these individuals to God, or are they drawing me away from Him?'

Where our work is, there let our joy be.

Commit your work to the LORD*,*
and your plans will be established.
Proverbs 16:3 NRSV

Legendary American college football coach Knute Rockne of Notre Dame University once achieved a marvellous performance from his team by urging them to 'Get out there, and win one for the Gipper,' a deceased former player. They gave their all for someone they cherished. How much more motivation can we muster by dedicating our efforts to God, the One who created us and loves us unconditionally?

Even on the days when the yearning for money, position, a boss's praise – or the fear of reprimand – do not motivate you at work, your love for your Heavenly Father should. In reality, God is your ultimate Boss, your ultimate Audience.

Whether you're doing something athletic, artistic, or career-oriented, do it for God. See Him as the One you serve, beyond your boss, your co-workers, your customers – or your own ambition. Dedicate the work to God in order to honour Him for the talents He gave you.

In serving God, you can't help but serve those around you – and you will know that you are doing the best you can do. However your efforts turn out, He will be proud of you, and you will know the joy of pleasing your Father. Give it all you've got – for the One who matters most.

If people can't be good Christians at work, they probably can't be good Christians anywhere.

Don't work hard only when your master is watching and then shirk when he isn't looking; work hard and with gladness all the time, as though working for Christ, doing the will of God with all your hearts.

Ephesians 6:6–7 TLB

In a massive opinion survey called 'The Day America Told the Truth', James Patterson and Peter Kim reported some shocking findings:

- Only 13 per cent of Americans saw all Ten Commandments as binding and relevant.
- Ninety-one per cent lied regularly, both at work and home.
- Most workers admitted to slacking off for an average of seven hours each week.
- About half of the work force admitted they regularly called in sick when they were in fact healthy.
- Further, when asked what they would be willing to do for 10 million dollars, 25 per cent said they would abandon their families, 23 pe rcent would be prostitutes for a week, and 7 per cent would murder a stranger.

Lest you attribute these results to non-Christians, researchers Doug Sherman and William Hendricks found that Christians were almost as likely as unbelievers to steal from the workplace, falsify their income-tax reports and disobey laws. And a University of Colorado professor conducted an experiment in which he gave students the opportunity to cheat. The Christian students cheated just as often as their non-Christian counterparts. 'I found no correlation between religiosity and honesty," the professor concluded.

To live a truly Christian life, one must do more than attend church and know all the right jargon. Following Christ is a 24-hour-a-day, 365-days-a-year mission-in all situations and under all circumstances.

I left my last occupation
due to illness and fatigue:
I got sick and tired
of that job!

A merry heart doeth good like a medicine.

Proverbs 17:22 KJV

America's Top Ten Worst Jobs

1. Macarena Instructor, Southern Baptist Convention
2. Mop boy, Sweatin' the Oldies Class
3. Tick and Flea Remover, Primate House, San Diego Zoo
4. Fan Mail Reader for Anson 'Potsie' Williams
5. Laundry Attendant, Chun's Sumo Wrestling Instruction School
6. Personal Trainer for Don Knotts
7. Barber for Don King
8. Javelin Catcher, US Olympic team
9. Personal Eyebrow Groomer for Andy Rooney
10. Porta-Potty Cleaner, Monster Truck Shows, Inc.

OK, you might not have the world's best job, but would you trade it for any of those listed above? And think about all the people who have no jobs. Sometimes it helps to look at work in its proper perspective. Consider what is good about your job, and be grateful for it.

(However, if any of the ten jobs above sound enticing, you should definitely consider a career change.)

Even the best racehorse
has to stop for oats
once in a while.

I will lie down and sleep in peace, for you alone, O Lord, make me dwell in safety.
Psalm 4:8

God doesn't sweat. He doesn't get tired or suffer with aching muscles. He never needs to take an aspirin. Yet what did He do after creating the world? He rested. He took the time to step back, cease working and enjoy His creation. If an all-powerful Being took the time to rest, that should speak volumes to us mere mortals.

We need to rest occasionally. We need to take time to recover physically, emotionally and spiritually from life's demands. We need time to take stock of where we've been, where we are and where we're headed. We need to take the time to be a friend, a parent, a child of God.

Various studies – including a very recent one at the University of Chicago – reveal that those who fail to recharge their mental and physical batteries once in a while are more susceptible to illness and stress-related problems such as ulcers – and to mistakes on the job. Many forget that activity, however productive it might seem, doesn't equal a quality life.

Additionally, in resting we find the time and the right frame of mind to contemplate God's wonders and to thank Him for His grace and kindness to us. We gather the energy to run the next miles on our journey with Him, and towards Him.

One has achieved
much who
has lived well,
laughed often,
and loved much.

Our mouths were filled with laughter,
our tongues with songs of joy.
Psalm 126:2

Be careful the next time you type up your CV, or fill out a job application. These people weren't careful enough!

- 'I have a graduate degree in unclear physics.'
- 'In my previous position, I saved the company $29,000 a year by removing ornamental pants from the reception area and the cafeteria.'
- 'My previous job was serving as a deceptionist in a lawyer's office.'
- 'My architectural experience includes designing golf curses.'
- 'I worked for twelve years as an uninformed security guard.'
- 'My volunteer experience includes delivering hot males to senior citizens.'
- 'I left my last job because my souse is in the Army and had to relocate.'
- 'I desire to work for a company that projects Judo-Christian values.'
- 'My last job was assistant manager at Walters Plumbing and Hating Specialists.'
- 'The academic scholarship I earned came with a $5,000 award and a plague.'
- 'Most of my experience to this point has been as a blue-color worker.'
- 'As part of the city maintenance crew, I repaired bad roads and defective brides.'
- 'After graduating from college, I worked in a clothing store for seven moths.'
- 'My career goal is to shave my talents with a growing company.'
- 'My hobbies include raising long-eared rabbis as pets.'

Dream no small dream.

'Seek, and ye shall find; knock, and it shall be opened unto you.'
Matthew 7:7 KJV

In 1970, Wally started baking chocolate chip cookies for his friends. He used a recipe and process passed down by his Aunt Della. For five years, he made cookies and gave away every batch – even though folks told him that his cookies were so good that he should sell them.

But to Wally, the cookies were just a sideline. His major goal was to be a big-time show business manager.

One day, a friend told Wally that she knew someone who could put up the money for a cookie-making business. That comment sparked Wally's thinking. He talked to some of his friends – people like Jeff Wall, Helen Reddy and Marvin Gaye – and convinced them to put up some money.

Originally, Wally intended to open only one shop, on Sunset Boulevard, just enough of a business to make a living. But Wally's enterprise grew faster and larger than he could have imagined. Soon, Wally's 'Famous Amos Chocolate Cookies' were being distributed worldwide.

Wally became a spokesperson for other products, including eggs and a telephone company. He had once dreamed of managing celebrities. Now he was one.

Sometimes dreams come through the back door. So keep it unlocked. You never know how the cookie is going to crumble.

Procrastination is the thief of time.

Make the most of every opportunity.

Colossians 4:5

Cindy, a young writer, grinned as she read her prose on the computer screen. The words were flowing smoothly from her brain to her fingers. *I'm even impressing myself,* she thought, a bit sheepishly. *This is the best short story I have ever written. Only a few more pages and I'll be done.*

She thought about pausing briefly to save her work, but she was on a roll. She feared the sudden inability to regain the rhythm she had found. *I'll save it as soon as it's finished, she reasoned.*

As Cindy plunged into the next paragraph, her cursor suddenly stopped blinking. Her pulse quickened. 'Come on,' she said, 'don't do this to me, please. Not now!' Cindy waited a few moments, then hit her space bar. Nothing. Panicking, she hit 'return'. No response.

Her screen was frozen like the arctic tundra.

She pounded furiously on her space bar and moved her mouse frantically across its pad, but she knew it was futile. *Why didn't I take a minute to save this?* she thought.

Cindy sighed deeply. All that appeared on the screen was the story title: 'Ready or Not'.

Cindy shook her head, then phoned her husband to tell him she'd be home late. Then she faced the almost-blank screen and began typing. Again.

Never, never,
never, never give up.

It is better to take refuge in the LORD than to trust in man.
Psalm 118:8

In the early 1900s Marian dreamed of becoming a concert singer. But she knew that because her skin was a different colour than that of the majority, she would be at a disadvantage.

Marian's dream was encouraged by her mother, who had a patient trust in God. Marian recalled, 'Mother's religion made her believe that she would receive what was right for her to have if she was conscientious in her faith. If it did not come, it was because He had not considered it right for her. We grew in this atmosphere of faith that she created. We believed as she did because we wanted the same kind of haven in the time of storm.'

When Marian was denied admission to a prestigious music conservatory because of her race, her mother calmly told her that 'someone would be raised up' to help her accomplish her goals. That someone arrived on the scene only a few weeks later. His name was Guiseppe Boghetti, one of Philadelphia's top voice teachers. He took Marian as a student.

Marian Anderson went on to become one of the twentieth century's most outstanding singers.

On Easter Sunday in 1939, she sang for more than 75,000 people, gathered, appropriately, at the Lincoln Memorial. Trusting her future to God, she achieved her dream – and beyond.

Wisdom is oft times nearer when we stop than when we soar.

As dead flies give perfume a bad smell, so a little folly outweighs wisdom and honour.

Ecclesiastes 10:1

Thomas flew a small aeroplane and often sold his services to hunters in the Canadian wilderness. One season he was approached by Jeb and Jake, two moose hunters. Thomas took them into the wild.

When Thomas returned to fetch his clients, he studied their gear and two gigantic moose.

'I'm sorry, fellas,' he told them, 'I can't fly out of here with the two of you, all your gear, and those two Bullwinkles!'

'Why not?' Jeb asked.

'Because the load will be too heavy for my plane. It will never get off the ground.'

'I don't understand this,' Jake said, exasperated. 'Last year each of us got a moose, and the pilot was willing to load everything on his plane.'

'Well,' Thomas said tentatively, 'I guess if the pilot did it last year, uh, I can too.'

They loaded up the plane, and Thomas fired the engines. The pontoon plane rose slowly and unsteadily. As it approached a mountain, it became apparent to Thomas that he would never clear this obstacle. Sure enough, the plane crashed partway up the mountain.

Fortunately, no one was hurt. As the trio crawled from the wreckage, Jeb asked, 'Where are we, Jake?'

Jake surveyed the area. 'Oh, about a mile farther than we got last year. Hey, Thomas, you're a better pilot than that last guy we had!"

Do not go where the path may lead; go instead where there is no path, and leave a trail.

'Everything is possible for him who believes.'

Mark 9:23

Some years ago, a large American shoe manufacturer sent two of its sales reps to different parts of the Australian outback. The company hoped that it could drum up some business among the Aborigines. It was a risky venture, but the firm realized how many new customers could be gained if the venture was successful.

After each rep had spent a few weeks in the outback, the shoe company received two faxes:

'There is no hope for new business here,' reported one rep. 'The Aborigines don't even wear shoes! It's not part of their culture. Couldn't we have researched this earlier and saved me the trip? This has been a colossal waste of time. I can't wait to get back home.'

The second rep filed a different report: 'Wow! What an incredible opportunity we have here in the outback! Did you know that Aborigines don't wear shoes at all? That means we have no competition from another manufacturer! We'll have thousands of new customers! Thanks for this great opportunity! It was an ingenious idea to send me here!'

As you can see, one person's obstacle is another person's opportunity. All it takes is some optimism and a little bit of soul (or sole).

Invest in knowledge.
The interest it earns will
astound you.

Wise men store up knowledge
Proverbs 10:14

Whether you are at secondary school pondering your future or you are in business considering a return to studying for a degree, or MA or PhD, here is some information worth considering. According to *Speaker's Idea File*, more Americans today (78 per cent) are high-school graduates than at any time in history. So, while a high-school diploma is a solid start, it doesn't distinguish one from the pack. Only 23 per cent of Americans have a degree beyond high school. Wherever you are, a university degree is a sound way to make you more competitive in the work force.

Education level also weighs heavily on the type of job a person gets and how much money she or he will make. Over the same time period, the average worker with a degree will earn twice the amount someone without a degree will earn. And you can double the number again for the average employee with a PhD.

If achieving the next educational level seems out of reach financially, consider checking into the many scholarships and grants available. And if the time commitment or scheduling seems overwhelming, there are many courses tailored specifically to the needs of people who must consider full-time work schedules and family.

Building on your educational foundation is worth considering. It won't just make you smarter, it will probably make you wealthier too.

To speak kindly does not hurt the tongue.

Since God so loved us, we also ought to love one another.

1 John 4:11

It's intriguing to watch how two different cultures approach a common business exercise.

The exercise involves pairing people off, placing or drawing a line between them, then instructing both members of the pair to convince the other to cross the line. The participants are allowed to use any persuasive means necessary – except physical force – to achieve their goal.

Americans attack the persuasion with vigour and ingenuity. They plead, cajole, intimidate, bargain, tempt, shame, berate and negotiate. However, for all their efforts, very few US players ever persuade their partners to cross the line.

Japanese business people take a different tack. One of them will simply and quietly say to his counterpart, 'If you will cross this line, so will I. That way, we both achieve our goals.' Then, each person crosses the line, and both win.

The business culture in the US is often marked by the familiar 'Looking out for Number One' approach. Often, even if we wish to distance ourselves from this way of achieving our career goals, we can find ourselves pulled into this way of thinking. Yet this mindset leaves everyone wanting. As our business world gets smaller, but also more complex, it's important to remember the effectiveness of co-operation.

It is hard to fail,
but it is worse
never to have
tried to succeed.

Lazy hands make a man poor,
but diligent hands bring wealth.
Proverbs 10:4

A vacationing couple in the California mountains happened upon a handsome young man sitting on a bridge near their resort hotel. Day after day they saw the man, sitting in the same spot. At first, they assumed he was a habitual fisherman, but upon taking a closer look, they realized he was doing nothing – just sitting and staring into space.

By the last day of their two-week vacation, the couple gave in to curiosity. 'Why do you sit in this one spot every day with apparently nothing to do?' they asked.

The young man replied with a smile, 'I believe in reincarnation. I believe that I have lived many times before and that I will have many lives following this one. So, I am sitting this one out.'

In the real world, people can't 'sit out' life as this obvious slacker was attempting to do. Each day, we either move closer to our goals or let them drift further from us. We get either stronger or weaker – mentally and physically. We either fortify our relationships or allow them to atrophy. You have only one chance to make today all that it can be – and only one chance to do something today that will make tomorrow better.

The happiest people don't necessarily have the best of everything; they just make the best of everything.

I have learned, in whatsoever state I am, therewith to be content. I can do all things through Christ which strengtheneth me.

Philippians 4:11,13 KJV

Two identical twins while similar in appearance were markedly different in attitude. The older twin was an optimist who was always smiling. But the younger brother was a pessimist who wore a perpetual scowl.

Concerned with the difference, the twins' parents took them to a psychologist in the hope that she might balance their personalities. The psychologist suggested that on their next birthday, the parents put the boys in separate rooms and give them their gifts.

'Give the pessimist the best toy you can find,' she advised. 'And give the optimist a box with some horse manure in it.'

The parents were puzzled, but they obeyed. They gave their sour son a popular action figure with a host of accessories. As they peeked in on him, they heard him whining, 'I hate this toy. It's the wrong colour. And I think I already lost some of the pieces! I bet my brother got something better.'

Tiptoeing to the sunny son's room, they found him eyeing the horse manure with a wide smile and bright eyes. 'This is so cool,' he shouted. 'Where there's manure, there's gotta be a pony nearby!'

Which twin do you resemble? Do you view life as a disaster waiting to happen – or a blessing about to be received?

Remember, the faith
that moves mountains
always carries a pick.

For as he thinketh in his heart, so is he.

Proverbs 23:7 KJV

As a high school senior, Jim averaged .427 as a baseball hitter – and also led his team in home runs. He quarterbacked his football team to the state finals. He later went on to pitch professionally in Major League Baseball.

Such feats would be remarkable for any athlete; for Jim they border on miraculous in that he was born without a right hand. As a quarterback, he had to handle snaps from centre with one hand. As a pitcher, he had to hurl the ball, then move his glove to his pitching hand in order to field. He had to catch ground balls or pop flies in his glove, then tuck the glove under his right arm, and retrieve the ball with his left hand before throwing it.

After one of his pro games, a boy approached Jim, who noticed immediately that the boy had only parts of two fingers on one of his hands. The boy shared that other kids called him 'Crab'.

'Kids used to tell me that my hand looked like a foot,' Jim told the boy. Then he asked an important question: 'Is there anything you can't do?'

'No,' came the reply.

'Well, I don't think so either,' Jim assured the boy.

Adversity causes some people to break, but it helps others to break records.

A clear conscience is a soft pillow.

Just say a simple yes or no, so that you will not sin.

James 5:12 TLB

Baylor University President Rufus C. Burleson once told an audience, 'How often I have heard my father paint in glowing words the honesty of his old friend Colonel Ben Sherrod. When he was threatened with bankruptcy and destitution in old age and was staggering under a debt of $850,000, a contemptible lawyer told him, "Colonel Sherrod, you are hopelessly ruined, but if you will furnish me five thousand dollars as a witness fee, I can pick a technical flaw in the whole thing and get you out of it."

'The grand old Alabamian replied, "Your proposition is insulting. I signed the notes in good faith, and the last dollar shall be paid if charity digs my grave and buys my shroud." '

It's the natural thing to want to find the easiest, least implicating means out of a tough situation. Yet what is at first difficult will be an asset later when people think about your integrity and character. The people you work with will remember you for the promises you keep and the truth you tell – especially at times when you could have profited from distorting or hiding the truth. Your character is your greatest asset, and your honesty is your most valuable currency.

Give to the world the best you have, and the best will come back to you.

A generous man will prosper; he who refreshes others will himself be refreshed.

Proverbs 11:25

The team of fry cooks was fried. They had spent all of a hot summer day in the sauna-like kitchen of a fast-food restaurant and hadn't even had time to break for lunch.

Late in the afternoon, business slowed down, and the restaurant manager walked into the kitchen to check on his employees. He noticed a box of chicken resting under the heat lamp.

'Did someone order this chicken?' he asked.

'Yes,' one of the cooks replied, 'but then he changed his mind.'

'Hmm,' the owner said. 'How about I give you this chicken at a 40 per-cent discount. Any takers?

The cooks looked at each other. They were ravenous, but at £5, that was about an hour's wages. Besides, the food was less than fresh.

'No takers, eh,' the manager grinned. 'OK, half-price. Final offer.'

The cooks again eyed each other, then shook their heads no.

'Fine,' the manager snapped. He tossed the box of chicken into the rubbish bin. 'I'm not giving my food away. Now get back to work.'

Every business must watch its bottom line, but be careful that money isn't too important to you. If you focus more on profits than on people, you may find yourself without the workers you need to run your business and make those profits.

Thinking is the hardest work there is, which is the probable reason so few engage in it.

A man is praised according to his wisdom.
Proverbs 12:8

Famed escape artist Harry Houdini issued a challenge wherever he went. He asserted that he could be locked in any jail cell in America, then free himself within minutes. He succeeded in city after city.

One time, however, something seemed to go wrong. Houdini entered a cell and heard the heavy metal door clang shut behind him. He took from his belt a concealed piece of strong but flexible metal and began to work on the lock to his cell. After a few minutes, he realized that something was wrong with this lock.

He worked for half an hour with no success. An hour passed. Houdini began to sweat and pant in exasperation. He manipulated his tool every way he could think of, but the lock wouldn't budge. After two hours, the frustrated magician leaned against the door in exhaustion. To his amazement, it swung open. His 'captors' had forgotten to lock it in the first place!

How many times do we make things harder than they have to be because we forget to stop, take stock of a situation and try the simple, most obvious solution? How many times are challenges impossible only because we think them to be so?

You're never in
worse company than
when you are
'beside yourself'.

A short-tempered man is a fool.
Proverbs 14:17 TLB

Marcus was letting his staff have it. He was furious that some key projects had gone uncompleted while he was away. As his tirade gained momentum, he began to swear and call his employees names. As he paused to catch his breath and loosen his tie, Marcus heard a child crying in the hallway.

'Oh, for Pete's sake!' he screamed, his temples throbbing. 'Can somebody go and shut that little brat up? We have a lot to talk about here, and that whining is going to drive me crazy!'

Katie, the administrative assistant, slipped out to attend to the matter while Marcus continued his assault.

A few minutes later, Katie slipped back into the room.

'Well, did you get the kid to shut up?'

Katie fidgeted in her chair and struggled to find the words to say.

With downcast eyes, Katie muttered, 'Not exactly, sir. Uh, the child in the hall is your daughter Megan. She came with your wife to visit you. She was crying because she heard you yelling.'

We all have bad days at work. But imagine if your children or spouse paid you a surprise visit on one of those days. If they witnessed how you react to stressful situations, how would you feel? More importantly, how would they feel?

Cheerfulness or joyfulness is the atmosphere under which all things thrive.

A happy heart makes the face cheerful.

Proverbs 15:13

An elderly pastor began a custom during his Sunday service – a custom he continued for twelve years. Before dismissing the children for Junior Church, he invited them all to the front of the sanctuary to march past his pulpit on their way to the special kid-oriented service.

As the kids walked past him, the pastor made a point to smile at each one. In return, all of them smiled at him. 'It was one of the high points of the service,' he once said.

One Sunday, however, the pastor became distracted during the Youth Exodus. He forgot to smile at one curly-haired, four-year-old girl. This girl left the line of children and ran back to her mother. Sobbing uncontrollably, she threw herself into her mother's arms.

After the service, the pastor sought out the mother to find out what had happened. She explained to him that, after her child had stopped crying, she said, 'Mummy, I'm so sad. I smiled at God, but he didn't smile back at me!'

The pastor reflected, 'To that child, I stood for God. I had failed with my smile, and the world went dark for her.'

Smile at each person you encounter at work today. It's doubtful that anyone will confuse you with God, but smiling is one way to express God's love.

A part of kindness consists of loving people more than they deserve.

Be kind and compassionate to one another.
Ephesians 4:32

Many years ago a child known as 'Little Annie' was locked in the dungeon of a mental institution near Boston – her doctors' last resort for the 'hopelessly insane'. At times, Annie seemed to fit the label. She was known to behave like an animal and viciously attack those who came near her 'cage'. At other times, she sat in a daze.

An elderly nurse, however, didn't see Annie as an animal. She began to take her lunch breaks outside Annie's cell. She hoped to find some way to communicate God's love to this troubled girl. One day, she left her dessert, a brownie, next to Annie's cell. Annie didn't acknowledge the gesture at the time, but when the nurse returned the next day, all that remained of the brownie were crumbs. From then on, the nurse brought Annie a brownie every Thursday.

As the months passed, the institution's staff noted changes in Annie's behaviour. She was removed to a more humane room. Ultimately, this once hopeless case was told she was able to return home.

Annie declined. A young adult by this time, she chose to stay at the institution to help others. One of the people she taught and nurtured was Helen Keller. As you've probably guessed, Annie's last name was Sullivan.

Worry is like a rocking-chair – it gives you something to do but gets you nowhere.

'Who of you by worrying can add a single hour to his life?'
Matthew 6:27

A businessman once made a 'Worry Chart', on which he recorded all his troubles and woes. After a year of this worrisome task, he decided to tabulate the results.

He found that 40 per cent of his anxieties turned out to be things that were unlikely to happen. Thirty per cent were about decisions he had made – and could not unmake. Twelve per cent of his worries were based on people's criticisms of him, and 10 per cent were about his future health (including getting an ulcer from too much worrying). Only half of the latter 10 per cent were items he had any control over. Finally, the businessman concluded that only 8 per cent of his past year's worries had been legitimate.

What are you worrying about today? How about converting your worry time to prayer time?

It's amazing how much worry can be alleviated when we talk to God about our concerns and, in effect, give them over to His care. And don't add worrying about how to pray to your list of concerns. If you can't find words to express your troubles, God knows your heart and mind and hears you even when you don't speak. Just sit quietly and soak up His goodness.

The only one who never makes mistakes is the one who never does anything.

Do not fear, for I am with you; do not be dismayed, for I am your God.

Isaiah 41:10

T. R. was having a terrible basketball game. He'd heard enough crowd taunts to last him all season. He just hoped he could avoid making any more mistakes.

His team was behind but gradually started to pull closer to the opposition. T. R. kept looking to the bench, expecting his coach to pull him from the game. But the coach stuck with his lineup.

Eventually, T. R. glanced at the scoreboard. His team was down by two points. Five seconds remained. T. R.'s team had the ball. Given his poor shooting percentage, he was sure no one would pass him the ball.

Wrong.

Because of his poor shooting average, T. R. found himself wide open just behind the half-court line. A teammate fired him the ball. He looked desperately for someone to pass to, but no one was open. As a defender charged him, T. R. fired an off-balance half-court shot in the general direction of the basket. The ball bounced hard off the backboard – and through the hoop.

As he accepted the congratulations from his teammates, T. R. didn't dare tell them that he almost didn't shoot the ball at all because he didn't want to face the prospect of missing.

He merely nodded and smiled the smile of a winner.

Be careful about letting it all hang out – you might not be able to get it tucked back in.

Keep your mouth closed and you'll stay out of trouble.

Proverbs 21:23 TLB

It was the company Christmas party, and several of the employees had put on sketches, which made the crowd applaud and roar with laughter. Morton, a company director, was feeling the warmth of too much holiday egg nog and found himself hungering for some of that applause.

Taking the stage, he grabbed a microphone and began to tell jokes. Off-colour jokes. At first, those in the audience sat in uncomfortable silence. Then, fearing they might anger him, they laughed politely. Encouraged by the response, Morton dipped deeper into his cache of inappropriate humour.

Mercifully, dessert was served, and Morton relinquished the microphone.

The following Monday, several employees visited human resources, reporting Morton for his inappropriate humour. When called in to explain himself, Morton dismissed the charges. 'My jokes weren't that bad,' he said. 'I think my accusers' memories were affected by drinking too much holiday cheer.'

Morton's episode could have become just another case of 'he said, she said', but it didn't. A friend of one of the employees featured in a sketch had videoed it, then left the recorder on during Morton's 'performance'. What happened to Morton next was no laughing matter.

Be careful what you say, especially at work. Words are like toothpaste. Once the stuff is out of the tube, you can't put it back in.

A visionary is one who can find the way by moonlight, and see the dawn before the rest of the world.

The vision is yet for an appointed time . . . it will surely come, it will not tarry.

Habakkuk 2:3 KJV

Eniac was one of the first computers to use electronic circuits, which allowed its users to make lightning-fast calculations. At first, Thomas Watson, former chairman of IBM, saw no use for this machine. He later recalled, 'It didn't move me at all. I couldn't see this gigantic, costly, unreliable device as a piece of business equipment.'

One day, though, Watson and his father wandered into an IBM research office and saw an engineer hook up a high-speed punch-card machine to a strange black box.

When asked what he was doing, the engineer said, 'Multiplying with radio tubes.' In simpler terms, the engineer's contraption was tabulating a payroll at one-tenth the time of a standard punch-card machine. 'That impressed me as though somebody had hit me on the head with a hammer,' Watson said. He told his father, 'Dad, we should put this thing on the market!'

That's how IBM got into electronics. Within a year, Big Blue had electronic circuits that multiplied and divided. Thousands of the IBM 604 were sold.

What wasn't immediately obvious to Thomas Watson was obvious to the engineer working in the research department. Always keep your eyes and ears open to those who work with you. They might just be on to something big.

Chance favours
the prepared mind.

Make the most of every opportunity.
Colossians 4:5

You can learn a lot from a moose. Each autumn during mating season, the Alaskan Bull Moose fights for dominance among its species. The moose battle head to head – literal-ly-crunching their 45-pound antlers together as they collide. When a moose has its antlers bro-ken, its defeat is ensured, for the antlers are essentially its only weapon.

In these battles, the moose with the largest and strongest antlers usually wins. Brain and skill have little to do with it. The victors are deter-mined the summer before mating season, when the moose eat nearly round the clock. The one that consumes the heftiest and healthiest diet will be the largest – with the most impressive antlers.

What is the lesson for us in the workplace and beyond? Battles are bound to flare up in our lives. We must equip ourselves ahead of time to ensure a victorious outcome. Just as Olympic athletes train for years to compete, we must be diligent to develop enduring character traits such as faith, strength and wisdom in order to prevail.

Now is the time to pray, read the Bible and work to develop strong character. When the bat-tle comes, you'll be a well-prepared warrior.

Good humour makes all things tolerable.

A merry heart doeth good like a medicine.

Proverbs 17:22 KJV

A manager encountered two rather dense fellows during a day of job interviews. He gave them each a task.

Later, the men met at a pizza place to compare notes.

'Boy, was that manager stupid!' exclaimed ignoramus No. 1. 'He gave me a five-dollar bill, then told me to go buy him a Porsche. The dummy didn't even tell me what colour he wanted!'

'You think that's bad,' replied ignoramus No. 2, 'we were doing the interview in this conference room, and he says, "Go up to my office, and see if I'm there. If I'm not there, come back and tell me." What a moron! There was a phone right there in the conference room. He could have called up to his office to see if he was there. He didn't have to send me!'

No. 1 shook his head sadly. 'I'm sure glad I didn't get the job. Who wants to work for an idiot?'

'I agree,' his companion said. Turning to the waitress, the first man asked for a pepperoni pizza.

'Would you like that cut into six or eight slices?' the waitress asked.

'Better make it six,' the second man replied. 'I don't think we're hungry enough for eight.'

You must look into people, as well as at them.

For you created my inmost being; you knit me together in my mother's womb.

Psalm 139:13

A medical-school professor once posed this medical/ethical question to his students: 'Here's a family history – the father has syphilis. The mother has TB. They already have four children. The first is blind. The second has died. The third is deaf. The fourth has TB. Now the mother is pregnant again. The parents come to you for advice. They are willing to abort their child if you decide they should. What do you say?'

After students shared various individual opinions, the professor placed them into groups to make final decisions. After deliberating, every group reported that it would recommend an abortion to the parents.

'Congratulations,' the professor told his class. 'You just took the life of Beethoven!'

What is the lesson for the workplace? A person's inherent value and potential don't depend on family background or social station. God has created each person with worth and skill and promise. The way we treat people on the job – and the decision of whom we hire – shouldn't be tainted by prejudice that's based on race, economic status, appearance or handicap.

This may seem like stating the obvious, but we might be surprised if we honestly evaluated the way we perceive others.

Every person has potential to add music to the great symphony called life.

The future belongs to those who believe in the beauty of their dreams.

Pleasant words are as a honeycomb, sweet to the soul, and health to the bones.

Proverbs 16:24 KJV

Shortly after arriving in Major League Baseball, pitcher Orel Hershiser was called to the office of Los Angeles Dodgers General Manager Tommy Lasorda. Hershiser feared the meeting wouldn't be pleasant. He had begun his career as a relief pitcher, and his performance had been disappointing.

Lasorda, however, didn't dwell on his pitcher's past. He said instead, 'You don't believe in yourself! You're scared to pitch in the big leagues! Who do you think these hitters are, Babe Ruth? Ruth's dead! You've got good stuff. If you didn't, I wouldn't have brought you up. You gotta go out there and do it on the mound. Be a bulldog – that's gonna be your new name. Bulldog Hershiser. I want you, starting today, to believe you are the best pitcher in baseball.'

Bulldog Hershiser wrote in his autobiography, *Out of the Blue*, 'I couldn't get over that Tommy Lasorda felt I was worth this much time and effort. He believed I had big league stuff.' In Hershiser's next game, he pitched three innings and gave up only one hit. He went on to have one of the longest pitching careers in recent Major League history.

As you talk with your employees and co-workers, focus more on their future than their past. All of us have much more potential than we have history.

Wise people speak when they have something to say; foolish people speak because they have to say something.

Let the words of my mouth, and the meditation of my heart, be acceptable in thy sight, O Lord.

Psalm 19:14 KJV

Need incentive to guard your tongue? Note these infamous quotes from some famous people:

- 'I was recently on a tour of Latin America, and the only regret I have was that I didn't study Latin harder in school so I could converse with those people.' – former US Vice President Dan Quayle
- 'China is a big country, inhabited by many Chinese.' – former French President Charles DeGaulle
- 'A verbal contract isn't worth the paper it's written on.' – film executive Samuel Goldwyn
- 'Half of this game is 90 per cent mental.' – baseball manager Danny Ozark
- 'We're going to turn this team around three-hundred and sixty degrees.' – basketball star Jason Kidd
- 'When more and more people are thrown out of work, unemployment results.' -former US President Calvin Coolidge
- 'Things are more like they are now than they ever were before.' – former US President Dwight Eisenhower
- 'It isn't the pollution that's harming the environment. It's the impurities in our air and water that are doing it.' – Dan Quayle
- 'The President has kept all of the promises he intended to keep.' – former Bill Clinton aide George Stephanopolous.

There is
no failure except in
no longer trying.

'Do not let you hearts be troubled. Trust in God.'
John 14:1

If you've been passed over for a promotion or a job, don't be too discouraged. Consider these:

- Michael Jordan, famous basket-ball player, was dropped from his high-school team.
- After his first screen test, Fred Astaire received the following assessment from an MGM executive: 'Can't act. Slightly bald. Can dance a little.'
- An American football 'expert' said of two-time Super Bowl winning coach Vince Lombardi, 'He possesses minimal football knowledge. Lacks motivation.'
- In screenings before test audiences, the pilot for *Seinfeld,* top-earning TV comedy, received low marks for its story line and main characters.
- Walt Disney was fired from a newspaper because he lacked ideas. Later, he went bankrupt several times before he built Disneyland.
- A young Burt Reynolds was told he couldn't act. His pal Clint Eastwood was told he would never make it in the movies because his Adam's apple was too big.

Certainly you can learn from rejection and disappointment. You may discover weaknesses you need to deal with to reach your maximum potential. Or the person making the assessment might be completely wrong. Let rejection fuel your determination. And hang on to those negative letters and reports. Someday, you might want to frame them.

A little nonsense now
and then is relished
by the wisest people.

Be joyful always.
1 Thessalonians 5:16

Coffee gets many of us going in the morning and picks us up from the afternoon doldrums. However, if we're not careful, we can become too dependent on the 'dark nectar'. Take the following self-test (put down that coffee mug first) and see how you rate. Circle those that apply to you.

Signs You're Coffee Co-dependent

- At company social gatherings, you don't mingle; you blend.
- You refer to your co-workers as your 'coffee mates'.
- If you had ten pence for every cup of coffee you have consumed – you'd buy more cups of coffee!
- If work gets stressful, you don't get mad. You get steamed.
- Most of your life's knowledge was gleaned from the backs of those little sugar packets.
- You gargle with coffee-flavoured mouthwash.
- You don't tan; you roast.
- The main reason you took your job: the coffee breaks.
- You think being called 'a drip' is a compliment.
- You can play ping-pong without an opponent.
- You named your cats Cream and Sugar.
- You go to bed early every night, so you can 'wake up and smell the coffee'.
- Your face is on the Colombian postage stamp.

We must learn to live together like brothers and sisters, or we will perish together like fools.

Live in harmony with one another.

1 Peter 3:8

Years ago, a rising public figure said, 'I am not nor have I ever been in favour of making voters or jurors of Negroes, nor of qualifying them to hold office, nor to intermarry with white people . . . There is a physical difference between the white and black races which I believe will forever forbid the two races living together on terms of social and political equality.'

In time, however, this man's views changed. Perhaps it was the courage and intelligence he saw 200,000 African American men display in battle. Perhaps the God he so often spoke of changed his mind, his heart. Whatever the case, four years after his racist statement, Abraham Lincoln issued the Emancipation Proclamation, clearing the path for the Thirteenth Amendment, which ended slavery in the United States.

Unfortunately, racism is still an evil that must be dealt with every day. Imagine how this must hurt God, who created us all and longs for us to live in harmony.

In your workplace, there are probably people from many ethnic backgrounds – people who reflect the rich diversity of an ingenious Creator. Remember, when God looks down on us, He only sees one race: the human race.

Do a good deed;
meet a need.

Be devoted to one another in brotherly love. Honor one another above yourselves.

Romans 12:10

Once, a young orphan girl, despondent and lonely, walked through a meadow and saw a small butterfly caught in a thorn bush. The more the butterfly struggled to free itself, the deeper the thorns cut into its fragile body.

Filled with compassion, the girl released the butterfly. But, instead of flying away, the butterfly transformed into an angel and said gently, 'To reward you for your kindness, I will do whatever you would like.'

The girl thought for a moment, then replied, 'I want to be happy!'

'Very well,' the angel said. Then the heavenly creature leaned close to the girl and whispered something in her ear.

Many years later, as the orphan lay on her deathbed after a full and happy life, her friends gathered around her. 'Won't you tell us your secret now,' they pleaded.

With a laboured smile, the woman answered, 'An angel told me that no matter where I went in life, I would find people who needed me – people rich or poor, young or old, meek or self-assured – and meeting those needs would bring me happiness and satisfaction.'

Somewhere in your workplace there is someone who needs you. Are you willing to be an angel and meet that need?

To earn honour is better than earning honours.

Them that honour me I will honour.

1 Samuel 2:30 KJV

Tension hung in the air. Rosalie Elliott had spelled her way to the fourth round of a national spelling competition in Washington, D.C. The eleven-year-old from South Carolina now faced the task of spelling the word 'avowal'. In her soft southern drawl, she began to recite the letters.

However, when she reached the next to last letter, the judges couldn't discern whether she said 'a' or 'e'. They debated among themselves for several minutes, listening to a tape of Rosalie's effort. The crucial letter, though, was simply too accent-distorted to decipher.

Finally, the lead judge sought input from the only person who could provide the answer. 'Was that second to last letter an "a" or an "e"?' he asked Rosalie. By this time, thanks to the whispering of her near-by competitors, Rosalie knew the correct spelling. Still, without hesitating, she replied that she had misspelled the word.

The entire audience – including some fifty newspaper reporters – stood and applauded. The moment was especially proud for her parents. Out of defeat, Rosalie had emerged a victor. And much more was written about her than the child who ultimately won.

Being a person of truth, even when the truth hurts, brings the greatest and most lasting rewards.

The beauty of character is a beauty that never fades.

The integrity of the upright shall guide them.

Proverbs 11:3 KJV

A Russian boy, plagued by feelings of ugliness, gazed into a mirror and studied his reflection – wide nose, thick lips, tiny grey eyes and over-large hands and feet. The boy was so distraught about his appearance that he begged God to work a miracle and turn him into a handsome man. He vowed that if God would transform him, he would give his Creator all that he now possessed and all that he would earn in the future.

That Russian boy was Count Tolstoy, who grew up to become one of the world's most revered authors. He is best known for his epic, *War and Peace*. In one of his books, Tolstoy reveals that through the years he discovered that the physical beauty he once craved is not the only beauty in life. Nor is it the best kind of beauty. Ultimately, Tolstoy grew to regard the beauty of a strong character as being most pleasing to God's eyes.

Many people today spend vast sums on their physical appearance. Expensive business suits. Tanning sessions at the spa. Gold watches. Cosmetic surgery. Character, in contrast, can't be bought or applied or worn. It is a matter of doing what's right, standing up for what's right. It's developing the qualities that you can't see by looking into the mirror.

You need not
have a lot to
give a lot.

'Anything is possible if you have faith.'

Mark 9:23 TLB

Some thought Les Goldberg crazy when he cashed in his personal investments to buy a home to lease to the homeless. But Goldberg, a retired engineer, felt that investing in the homeless would bring rich dividends – just not monetary ones.

Goldberg retired from his job to a life of service. He works on six service boards and leads a team of homeless people on various odd jobs and charity work. He has never regarded the homeless as irresponsible or unreliable. He sees them simply as people. And the home that he bought is used as a temporary homeless shelter and a drop-in centre – a place where homeless people can pick up their mail, make phone calls, pursue job leads, and receive donated goods.

At any given time, four homeless people live at the house, paying a small rent to help offset expenses. And house rules are strict: no alcohol, no drugs and no loitering.

Les Goldberg, by the way, is not some wealthy philanthropist who gives from his abundant resources. Prior to retiring, he worked for twenty years designing and installing fire sprinklers. His annual income was about $25,000 a year. Goldberg is simply a man who saw a need and found a way to meet it.

Brush up on your honesty; it will help you fight truth decay.

A truthful witness gives honest testimony,
but a false witness tells lies.
Proverbs 12:17

Four young consultants competed vigorously for a newly-vacated management position at a large investment firm. After carefully considering each candidate's merits, a team of executives made its decision. They decided to notify the lucky consultant of his promotion after lunch.

During the lunch hour, one of the directors spotted the manager-to-be ahead of him in line at the company cafeteria, separated by several other customers. The director watched the young man select his food, including a small square of butter. As soon as the candidate placed the pat of butter onto his plate, he quickly placed a dinner roll on top of it to hide it from the cashier.

That afternoon, the executive team met in the boardroom, then summoned the deceitful young man. He walked to the boardroom, full of hope. He imagined his large new office, the substantial raise, his own administrative assistant and the management bonus. However, rather than promote the candidate, the management team fired him.

Honesty isn't a selective quality. People who lie about small matters tend to lie about larger ones as well. So invest in honesty. You and those you work with will love the dividends that truth brings.

You can't do much about your ancestors, but you can influence your descendants tremendously.

As for me and my house,
we will serve the LORD*.*

Joshua 24:15 KJV

Bill Galston had reached the peak of his career when he resigned as domestic policy advisor to President Clinton to return to teaching at the University of Maryland. His reason for leaving his high-profile, high-influence post? 'To strike a new balance between work and family.'

Danny Ainge offered similar reasons for stepping down as head coach of the Phoenix Suns, one of the National Basketball Association's hottest young teams.

Both men had achieved great things in their respective careers, but both ultimately had to face the fact that their jobs kept them away from their families. And when they were home, they were often too tired and stressed-out to truly enjoy the time.

The choices you make will affect more than your future; they will impact the future of your children. Make sure you have your family's best interest in mind as you make choices on the job. If you are talented at what you do, you will probably have lots of time to achieve career goals. In fact, you might change careers several times before you retire – and be successful each time.

Your children, however, will be young only once.

Don't sacrifice your health for the sake of wealth.

People who want to get rich fall into temptation and a trap and into many foolish and harmful desires that plunge men into ruin and destruction.

1 Timothy 6:9

Follow these ten simple steps, and you can have your very own full-blown ulcer, just like many of the other movers and shakers in your workplace. And if you act quickly, you get a bonus case of fatigue and burnout at no extra charge!

1. On the job, be driven to make more money, faster than all your peers.

2. Eat sporadically. Skip breakfast-just have a cup of coffee instead. In fact, replace as many meals as possible with a caffeine – or sugar-loaded drink.

3. Try to work up a hefty rage every chance you get. Always give full vent to your anger.

4. Worry about everything. And don't pray about anything.

5. Don't take holidays. After all, they're for wimps. And don't forget to take work home regularly.

6. Ignore minor physical symptoms, such as abdominal pain, nausea or dizzy spells. Be tough.

7. Always stick to your opinion like superglue. Don't entertain the notion that you might sometimes be wrong. Keep your opinion rigid at all times.

8. Never delegate responsibility. Do it all yourself, and do it perfectly.

9. Don't sleep for eight hours a night. You can get by on four or five. You can always drink coffee if you feel tired during the workday. And wear those bags under your eyes like little puffy badges of valour.

10. Do not, under any circumstances, relax. Somebody might get ahead of you and grab the credit you deserve.

Remember, the faith that moves mountains always carries a pick.

Be very careful, then, how you live—not as unwise but as wise, making the most of every opportunity.

Ephesians 5:15–16

There's nothing wrong with testing the job market occasionally, but some people take job-hopping to the extreme, moving from one position to another with the frequency of short-wave radio transmissions.

Try this experiment next time you're in a large group. Unwrap an adhesive bandage and apply it to your arm. Then peel it off and have the person next to you do the same. Then pass it on to the next person. It won't take long for the bandage to lose most of its bonding ability. Soon, it will not be able to adhere at all.

The same thing can happen to job-hoppers. They never give themselves time to bond with a company's mission or its employees. The job-hopper always has the next move on his or her mind, making it difficult to concentrate on the job at hand. It's difficult for someone of this mentality to achieve any sense of job satisfaction.

No one should stay in a dead-end job, but if your current position inspires and challenges you, don't be afraid to stick with it, even if it's occasionally unfulfilling or tedious. Instead of dreaming about the next 'opportunity', find ways to keep your position fresh.

And when it comes to wanting more challenge in a job, it never hurts to ask.

Industry is fortune's right hand.

A man is praised according to his wisdom.

Proverbs 12:8

Forbes magazine reported on the Home Depot shopping chain and the reasons behind its success. One example: Home Depot surveyed its customers, asking them, among other things, which brand of water heater they had in their homes.

General Electric rated as the third most popular brand. There was only one problem with this response. GE doesn't make water heaters. Home Depot management could have spent lorry-loads of advertising money re-educating its customers about who produces water heaters. But they had a better idea. They decided to make their customers right.

Home Depot struck an agreement with Rheem, a large company that *does* make water heaters, and GE. Home Depot bought quantities of Rheem heaters, then placed GE stickers on them.

Everybody won. Rheem got greater product exposure in a giant chain of stores. GE earned a licensing fee for the use of its name on the product – not to mention follow-up business in parts and service. Home Depot became exclusive distributors of GE/Rheem water heaters. And customers gained an opportunity to buy one of their favourite brands of water heater - even though that favourite was non-existent before.

Many of us limit our achievements because we focus on what exists (or how things have always been done). Those who achieve success are willing to stretch their necks out to see beyond the norm.

Happiness is a perfume
you cannot pour
on others without
getting a few drops
on yourself.

Honour one another above yourselves.

Romans 12:10

Author and literary agent Chip MacGregor discovered something intriguing while doing research on English literature. It seems that in the early 1900s, American author Sherwood Anderson spent years of his life coaching and mentoring other writers. He lived near them, dined with them, read their writings and encouraged them to communicate more effectively and powerfully.

One of Anderson's first pupils was Ernest Hemingway. John Steinbeck also studied under him, as did William Faulkner, the greatest novelist the South has ever produced. In all, Anderson's pupils included four Pulitzer Prize winners and five National Book Award honorees.

Malcolm Cowley, considered by many to be the pre-eminent editor of our time, said, 'No one has influenced the novel of the twentieth century more than Sherwood Anderson.' Ironically, Anderson was a rather obscure novelist in his own right. Only one of his works, *Winesburg, Ohio*, is widely known – and that only among English literature majors and teachers.

Perhaps you are a person who can mentor others and help them to achieve high-profile success. The rewards you earn might not burn as brightly as you would like, but they will last. And they will bring you a deep sense of satisfaction. It's a noble task to help others fulfil their dreams.

The mightiest oak
tree was once just
a little nut that
stood its ground.

Lazy hands make a man poor,
but diligent hands bring wealth.
Proverbs 10:4

Magazine publisher Gerhard Gschwandtner recently paid tribute to the venerable newspaper the *New York Times.* In his tribute, Gschwandtner noted that when publisher Adolph Ochs took over the *Times* back in 1896, it was a struggling little paper competing with more than a dozen other New York dailies. It had a paltry nine thousand subscribers.

Once at the helm of this floundering ship, Ochs promptly lowered its retail price from three cents to a single penny and vowed to publish the news 'impartially, without fear or favor'. Then he cut out the paper's fiction section, as well as columns he deemed stale.

His slogan for his publication became 'All the news that's fit to print'. He launched a Sunday magazine with photographs to provide diversity and visual appeal.

By increasing value while decreasing price, Ochs quickly boosted the *Times*' circulation to 350,000 – an astounding 39-fold growth. And by the late 1990s, the paper that once sold for only a penny was a $1.7 billion company – with 79 Pulitzer Prizes to its credit.

So don't be discouraged if your company is small or struggling. By focusing on value and quality, you can turn things around. And that's good news that's fit to print anywhere.

Sometimes we get so busy adding up our troubles that we forget to count our blessings.

Be very careful, then, how you live-not as unwise but as wise, making the most of every opportunity.

Ephesians 5:15–16

Five Rules for a Happy Day on the Job:

1. Today I will not strike back. If a co-worker or customer is rude, impatient or unkind, I will not respond in a like manner.
2. Today I will ask God to bless my enemies. If I encounter a longtime business rival or difficult customer – or anyone who treats me harshly or unfairly – I will quietly ask God to bless him or her.
3. Today I will be careful about what I say. I will carefully choose and guard my words, making certain that I don't spread gossip or malign anyone in any way.
4. Today I will go the extra mile. I will find ways to share another's burdens. I will find ways to make life more pleasant for everyone I encounter.
5. Today I will forgive. I will forgive the hurts and injuries that come my way today. And I will try to put past hurts and insults behind me, once and for all.

Once you've had time to digest these rules for a happy work day, turn the page and find five more. These ideals may seem a little lofty, but they are guaranteed to help you keep your attitude straight and your work relationships rightly aligned.

It's not hard to make decisions when you know what your values are.

The just man walketh in his integrity: his children are blessed after him.
Proverbs 20:7 KJV

Five More Rules for a Happy Day on the Job:

1. Today I will do something nice for someone, but I will do it secretly. I will reach out anonymously to bless the life of another person.
2. Today I will treat others as I wish to be treated. I will practise the golden rule – do unto others as you would have them do unto you – with everyone I meet.
3. Today I will raise the spirits of someone who is discouraged. My smile, my words, my expressions of hope and support – all can make a difference to someone who is struggling with discouragement or depression.
4. Today I will nurture my body. I will eat less. I will eat healthy foods. My staples will not be coffee and doughnuts. I will be grateful for, and respectful of, my body.
5. Today I will grow spiritually. I will use breaks, lunch and quiet times to pray and meditate. I will seek a quiet place, a quiet moment, so that I can rejuvenate myself spiritually.

There are difficult people in every workplace. Those who tear others down to build themselves up. Resist the urge to stoop to their standard. Instead, rise above it by aligning yourself with God's standard.

Be wiser than other people if you can, but do not tell them so.

A discerning man keeps wisdom in view.

Proverbs 17:24

British prime minister Winston Churchill had just finished a rousing speech. Upon his final words, the crowd gathered to hear him erupted with thunderous applause. When the clapping and cheering faded, one man, unimpressed by Churchill's rhetoric, blew him 'a raspberry'. The rest of the audience sat in suspense, awaiting the powerful statesman's response to the rude man.

Churchill looked at his tormentor and spoke, 'I know. I agree with you. But what are we among so many?'

Churchill's reply was a hit with the throng, and a potentially tense situation was diffused.

Like Sir Winston, you may occasionally face insults or someone who openly opposes your position on an issue – perhaps in a condescending manner. It's tempting to become angry and lose your composure. Many of us have been led to believe that, in order to show our strength, we must fight fire with fire. But don't forget the power of humour and humility when dealing with criticism or rudeness.

The Bible promises that a soft answer turns away wrath. Certainly there will be times when you must forcefully defend yourself or your position on an important work-related issue. Be watchful, however, for the times when fighting fire with fire will only make everyone hot and miserable and do nothing to resolve the situation.

The race is not
always to the swift,
but to those who
keep on running.

Do not conform any longer to the pattern of this world, but be transformed by the renewing of your mind.

Romans 12:2

We live in an age marked by immediate gratification. We have instant coffee, microwave dinners and instant messaging. Today, first-class mail is called 'snail mail'. There's overnight delivery for nearly anything we may need (or want) to purchase.

However, there is no 'Instant Formula' for career success, despite what you might hear. Many have chased get-rich-quick dreams, only to discover disappointment – and a lighter wallet. Becoming good at your job takes time. Time to learn new skills and refine old ones. Time to make a few mistakes, then learn from them. Time to understand your job and the jobs of those who work with you.

So don't try to climb the corporate ladder or launch a business too quickly; if the ladder isn't secure, you might slip and fall. Realize that becoming good at anything is a process.

Learn to enjoy that process. Enjoy learning. Enjoy your co-workers, especially those who can help you grow personally and professionally. Enjoy the confidence you build day by day as you become better and better at what you do.

Remember, a career path is like a marathon course, not a fifty-metre dash.

The greatest use of life
is to spend it for
something that
will outlast it.

The fear of the LORD teaches a man wisdom, and humility comes before honour.

Proverbs 15:33

To some people, the workplace is about power, clout and money. They strive to have the biggest offices, the largest salaries and the heftiest benefits package. They want to be at all the important meetings and social functions – dressed in the most expensive clothes.

There's nothing wrong with achieving success in your job or advancing in the company. But remember that God is the ultimate CEO, and His standards for success differ markedly from those of the power brokers and image seekers.

In the Bible, we find principles like these: The last shall be first, and the first shall be last. A small seed becomes a great tree. One lost sheep takes priority over the rest of the entire flock. The Bible encourages people to 'walk humbly'. And as we walk humbly, we become more in tune with God's character. We become more concerned with who we can help and encourage rather than who we can step on during our climb to career greatness.

How do you want to be remembered when you retire? Would you like to be thought of as the person who always had a smile for discouraged co-workers? How about the one who never hesitated to take on any job, no matter how menial it seemed? The decision is yours.

Every person is
my teacher; I learn
something from
everyone that I meet.

Enter not into the path of the wicked,
and go not in the way of evil men.
Proverbs 4:14 KJV

A middle manager who was confronted with frequent ethical dilemmas or problems was fond of saying, 'What would Phil do?' Whether in large meetings or one-on-ones, when a problem would arise, she would thoughtfully utter those four words. This behaviour piqued the curiosity of the manager's colleagues.

After a blistering debate about downsizing, one of them spoke up: 'OK, I have to ask you – you repeatedly say, "What would Phil do?" whenever you're confronted with a difficult issue. Who is Phil? He must be a very wise man if you consider his example whenever you have to make an important decision. Was he one of your mentors?'

The manager laughed and shook her head. 'Mentor is probably not the best term,' she noted.

'Phil was a former manager of mine – a completely unprincipled, profane and egotistical man. He rarely made a good decision, and even his few good decisions weren't made for the right reasons. So, when I ask myself "What would Phil do?" I consider the answer. Then I do exactly the opposite. That formula has yet to fail me.'

If you must work for unprincipled or incompetent managers, realize that you can learn as much from them as from a great leader.

God give me work
till my life shall end
and life till my
work is done.

A happy heart makes the face cheerful.
Proverbs 15:13

You Know It's Time to Retire When –

- You try to straighten out the wrinkles in your socks and realize you aren't wearing any.
- At the breakfast table before work, you hear lots of 'Snap, Crackle and Pop', but you're not eating cereal.
- Your back goes out, but you stay home.
- You wake up looking like your passport photo.
- It takes you two or three tries to get up from your chair.
- You take a holiday, and your energy runs out before your money does.
- The only birthday gift you want from your co-workers is not to be reminded of your age.
- Your idea of weight-lifting is standing up after a long meeting.
- It takes longer to rest than it does to get tired.
- Your memory keeps getting shorter, but your list of complaints gets longer.
- Most of the names in your phone book start with 'Dr'.
- You sit in a rocking chair but can't get it started.
- Getting ready for work, you find it takes you twice as long to look half as good.
- Your colleagues compliment you on your patience, but you know the secret is that you just don't care any more.

No one is useless who lightens the burdens of another.

Pleasant words are as a honeycomb, sweet to the soul, and health to the bones.

Proverbs 16:24 KJV

Ten Commandments of Harmonious Employee Relationships

1. Don't forget to say hello. Few things make co-workers feel as wanted and happy as a cheerful, sincere greeting.
2. Smile. It takes only four muscles, but the lift it provides others can be massive.
3. Call people by their names – their correct names. It makes them feel valued.
4. Offer to help. It may be just what someone needs to keep from being overwhelmed or discouraged.
5. Make eye contact. Don't be too busy to look at colleagues, not beyond them to your next task or destination.
6. Be generous with praise, cautious with criticism.
7. Be public with praise, private with criticism.
8. Be considerate and wise during disagreements. There are often three sides to an argument: your side, your adversary's side and the right side.
9. When in doubt as to whether you should say something, DON'T. There is probably a good reason for your hesitation.
10. Have a sense of humour. It's the safety valve that keeps work from being a dangerous pressure cooker.

If thou keepest these commandments, then shalt thou be blessed in thy office, blessed in thy hallway, blessed in thy break room, blessed even, yea and lo, in thy parking lot.

There is a word for leaders who won't correct their associates: miserable.

Rebuke a wise man and he will love you. Instruct a wise man and he will be wiser still.

Proverbs 9:8–9

Walking through a heavily wooded national park, a man saw a large tree that was growing crooked. Near the tree, someone had placed a large upright pole and tied it to the tree with ropes in an effort to help straighten it. Unfortunately, the upper part of the tree had grown out so far from its trunk that there was no way to correct the misdirected growth. The crooked part of the tree was too far from the corrective pole.

The same phenomenon can happen to business leaders. Some of them let their employees run wild during their early days on the job – not wanting to correct them and risk hurting their morale or causing them to leave the company. But, before long, these managers find that they can't correct the wayward associates, even with help from an outside source. Employees require regular and consistent direction and, occasionally, correction when they have violated company policy or made a poor decision. Such leadership creates clear expectations and shows employees that someone cares about them enough to help them keep their careers (and the company) on the right path.

So, if you see behaviour that troubles you and might damage your company, your employees or your customers, take action – delivered with careful consideration and tact.

The greatest quality that an individual can possess is the ability to get along with others. It is a quality that I am willing to pay more for than any other.

Live in harmony with one another.

1 Peter 3:8

Andrew Carnegie was able to assemble the greatest private-enterprise leadership team of his day. To accomplish this goal, he searched the world for the top men and women in their various fields of expertise.

At one point, he found a chemist in Germany who was the best of the best. Carnegie more than doubled his salary, and he gave him a new house and a five-year contract. However, three months later, Carnegie called the chemist into his office and fired him. He bought out the rest of his contract and paid his moving expenses back to Germany.

Why forfeit such a substantial investment and fire an elite scientist? Because, as Carnegie discovered, this chemist was impossible to get along with. He constantly argued with others on the leadership team and hindered their progress.

Explaining his decision, Carnegie strongly declared, 'I will not have anyone work for me, especially in a leadership position, who does not have the quality of being able to get along with others.'

Expertise in your field will get you only so far in your career. Don't develop and practise your technical skills at the expense of people skills. Or, as another Carnegie, Dale, might put it, don't discount the value and necessity of 'making friends and influencing people'.

The future is purchased by the present.

Do not be wise in your own eyes.
Proverbs 3:7

A trade association excitedly put together a mass mailing advertising its new products and services. One executive looked over the materials and declared them ready to send to the printer, then on to thousands of customers.

'Shouldn't we have someone in the editorial department look this over for errors?' an administrative assistant asked.

'No way,' the executive snorted. 'I can't stand those picky people. They're always quibbling about the grammatical errors in our stuff and driving me crazy! Who cares about a misplaced comma here or there? We have to get this mailing out next week. We can't afford any delays!'

So, the mailing went to the printer, then on to the association's vast mailing list of current and prospective customers. The association beefed up its inbound telephone customer service staff in anticipation of increased business. But the company was puzzled when no calls came in about the mailing. Within a couple of weeks, an editorial staff member found a copy of the brochure that was the main part of the mailing.

'Hey,' she said to the editor-loathing executive, 'did you know that you have our order number wrong in this brochure?'

As this association learned the hard way, it's never a good idea to short-cut quality control – or disregard the expertise of fellow workers.

To appreciate nonsense requires a serious interest in life.

He will yet fill your mouth with laughter and your lips with shouts of joy.

Job 8:21

Fifteen Irrefutable Pearls of Business Wisdom

1. Before you criticize co-workers, walk a mile in their shoes. That way, if they get angry, they'll be a mile away – and barefoot.
2. A clear conscience is often the sign of a bad memory.
3. It is almost always easier to get forgiveness than permission.
4. For every action, there is an equal and opposite government plan.
5. Age is a very high price to pay for wisdom and maturity.
6. Bills travel through the post at twice the speed of cheques.
7. Men are from earth. Women are from earth. Deal with it.
8. Middle management is the point at which broadness of the mind and narrowness of the waist change places.
9. Opportunities always look bigger going than coming.
10. Junk is something you throw away three weeks before you need it.
11. There is always one more imbecile than you counted on.
12. Artificial intelligence is no match for natural stupidity.
13. Experience is a wonderful thing. It enables you to recognize a mistake when you make it again.
14. By the time your business can make ends meet, someone moves the ends.
15. Blessed are they who can laugh at themselves, for they shall never cease to be amused.

Opportunity is missed by most people because it is dressed in overalls and looks like work.

The plans of the diligent lead to profit as surely as haste leads to poverty.

Proverbs 21:5

After five years as a sales manager, Amanda could proudly state that she had reached her quarterly sales goals every time. Her territory had grown to include the entire American state in which she lived. And she had built an excellent reputation among her peers and competitors.

Then, suddenly, she was assigned to a neighbouring state. Amanda was dismayed to learn that her predecessor hadn't worked very hard, so the territory was undeveloped. Assessing her new position, Amanda decided she had been demoted. Her first impulse was to reign.

Instead, she reasoned that hard work had produced results in the past, so why not try it now? She put in long hours and lots of miles during the next few months. And, by the end of the third quarter, her results surpassed those she had enjoyed in her previous territory!

She had turned a trial into a triumph.

The company rewarded Amanda by naming her a regional vice president, with a territory that included both her former and current states. Had she stayed with the old position, Amanda wouldn't have been able to prove her ability to turn around a poor territory, and she wouldn't have earned her promotion.

So, learn from Amanda, and keep your hand to the plough. You never know how fertile even the roughest soil may be!

One good head is better than a hundred strong hands.

The discerning heart seeks knowledge.
Proverbs 15:14

In 1935 Thomas Dewey was appointed special prosecutor for New York City. His job was to identify the structures behind organized crime in New York, trace the evidence and dethrone Mafia leadership. One of the lawyers Dewey hired for his team was a woman named Eunice Carter. An expert on the Harlem district, Carter was assigned to look into illegal numbers games in that part of the city. Carter was also responsible to prosecute other low-level crimes, such as street prostitution.

It was in these 'side' duties that Carter began to notice a pattern. Defendants in various vice cases told curiously similar stories. The same law firm was making frequent appearances – and the same bondsmen paying bail. Carter doubted these patterns could be coincidence. Dewey assigned detectives to work with Carter. A court order was issued, telephone lines were tapped, suspects were followed.

On Saturday night, February 1, 1936, 160 plainclothes police officers were dispatched. At exactly 9:00 p.m., eighty houses throughout New York City were raided. The evidence secured in this bust exposed and shut down the extensive crime reign of Mafia kingpin Charlie 'Lucky' Luciano.

When tracking an unseen problem, watch for patterns. They will often lead you to the source of the trouble-whether you're fighting crime, declining sales or lost productivity.

Few things are as
powerful as an idea
whose time has come –
and few things as
frustrating as an
idea whose time
has not yet come.

*The plans of the diligent lead to profit
as surely as haste leads to poverty.*
Proverbs 21:5

A college senior basketball player finished his career with a flourish. He racked up impressive statistics, won several post-season honours and led his team into the NCAA tournament. All he had to do was make a decent showing at a spring camp, and he was certain to be a No. 1 draft choice in the NBA.

Unfortunately, he broke his nose before the camp. He had to reduce his training regime and wear a protective face guard. He thought about skipping the camp and giving himself time to heal. But he decided to attend. He even removed his face guard because he didn't want the scouts to think he was 'soft'. Unfortunately, as he scrimmaged with other NBA hopefuls, the ex-college star couldn't take his mind off his aching – and vulnerable – nose. He played tentatively and passively. The scouts in attendance wrote him off as a top prospect. And when the first-round draft picks were called off weeks later, this player's name was not among them.

The lesson: First impressions are lasting. In today's business climate, there is constant pressure to be 'first to market'. However, in our haste we should never forget that there's nothing to be gained from being first to market with inferior product, poor customer service or weak marketing support. In an effort to be timely, don't be too early. It just might help you 'save face'.

The dons are too busy educating the young to be able to teach them anything.

Be joyful always.
1 Thessalonians 5:16

Things They Probably Didn't Teach You at Business School

- Always remember, you are special and unique. Just like everyone else.
- Never test the depth of the water with both feet.
- It is far more impressive when others discover your good qualities without your help.
- If you tell the truth, you don't have to remember so much.
- If you lend a co-worker £20 and never see that person again, it was probably worth it.
- The 'good' things that come to those who wait are what's left behind by those who got there first.
- Never underestimate the power of stupid people in large committees.
- Good judgment comes from bad experience, and a lot of that experience comes from bad judgment.
- The quickest way to double your money is to fold it in half and put it back in your pocket.
- There are two theories about arguing with female co-workers. Neither one works.
- Never miss a good chance to shut up.
- Generally speaking, you aren't learning much when your mouth is moving.
- Anything worth taking seriously is worth making fun of.
- Diplomacy is the art of saying 'good doggie' while looking for a big stick.
- The older you get, the better you get (unless you're a banana).

Happiness is not
a destination,
but a journey.

Keep your lives free from the love of money and be content with what you have.

Hebrews 13:5

An expert wood carver sat on his front porch, sipping lemonade and enjoying the view one spring afternoon. Around him on the porch sat his various creations. A friend of his stopped by for a quick visit and was surprised to see the artisan relaxing. 'It's only 1:30 in the afternoon,' he observed, 'a little early for a break, isn't it?'

The artisan swallowed a mouthful of lemonade and yawned. 'This isn't a break,' he said. 'I'm done for the day.'

His friend, a young marketing executive, was nonplussed: 'What do you mean? It's too early in the day to stop. You need to produce more! If you carve more figures, you can make more money. You could even hire an assistant to help you with the business end of things. You could buy new tools. You could buy a shop, so you wouldn't have to carve here at your house.'

'Why would I want to do all of that?' the carver asked.

'So you can make more money!' his friend spluttered.

'And what would I do with all that extra money?'

'Why – enjoy life, of course!'

The wood carver took another sip of lemonade, leaned back in his chair, and closed his eyes. Before he drifted off for a nap, he mumbled contentedly, 'What do you think I'm doing?'

Do not look
where you fell,
but where you slipped.

Be very careful, then, how you live – not as unwise but as wise.
Ephesians 5:15

A man was brought to trial for illegal possession of drugs. His chances didn't look good. He was caught red-handed while being stopped for a traffic offence.

The police had spotted the drugs lying in plain sight in the man's vehicle. And he had a previous drug conviction. However, as the defence attorney examined the papers related to the arrest and subsequent criminal charges, he smiled, whispered to his client, then approached the presiding judge. The defence lawyer pointed out that whoever had typed up the papers had misspelled the name of the drug the defendant allegedly had in his car. The erroneous spelling constituted the name of a narcotic, but not the one the defendant had been caught with. Thus, he argued, the case had to be thrown out. His client was never in possession of the drug listed in the official documents.

So, due to a lack of attention to detail, a guilty man went free, and a police officer's work went for naught.

While the situation may not be as extreme, failing to take the details into account in your job can have severe consequences, especially on the back side of a project. If you think details don't matter, just ask a lucky law-breaker. Or an angry cop.

There is none so foolish as the one who thinks himself or herself abundantly wise.

He that walketh with wise men shall be wise: but a companion of fools shall be destroyed.

Proverbs 13:20 KJV

How well do you solve problems on the job? This brief quiz will help you gauge (and improve) your problem-solving ability. The questions seem simple, but think carefully before answering.

1. How do you put a giraffe into the fridge?
2. How do you put an elephant into the fridge?
3. The Lion King is hosting an animal conference. One animal is missing – which one?
4. You come to a river that is known to be inhabited by crocodiles. How do you get across?

1. **Answer:** Open the fridge, jam in the giraffe and close the door.

Point: Do you tend to do simple things in an overly complicated way?

2. **Answer:** Open the fridge, take out the giraffe, put in the elephant and close the door. Did you remember to remove the giraffe?

Point: This tests your ability to think through the repercussions of your actions.

3. **Answer:** The elephant because it's still in the fridge!

Point: How good is your memory and sense of continuity?

4. **Answer:** You can swim across safely. All the crocodiles are at the Lion King's animal conference.

Point: How good is your ability to learn quickly from previous mistakes?

If you didn't fare well on this quiz, don't despair. About 90 per cent of business professionals incorrectly answered all four questions. Children, on the other hand, usually answered them all correctly.

Delayed obedience
is disobedience.

A wise man will hear, and
will increase learning.
Proverbs 1:5 KJV

Major General Charles Lee was the most seasoned officer on George Washington's staff. Early in the American Revolution, Washington instructed Lee to take his forces north. Washington sent a second letter, then a third, but Lee continued to delay. Irritated, Washington wrote: 'My former letters were so full and explicit that I expected you would have been sooner in motion.' Still, Lee found reasons to procrastinate.

Finally, Lee began to move, but he suggested he would lend greater aid by remaining on the British rear to harass them from behind. Washington wrote back, 'I cannot but request and entreat you to march and join me with all your whole force, with all possible expedition.'

Still, Lee chose to do his own thing. Then, while eating breakfast in a tavern one morning, unprotected and unprepared, British troops found him and captured him. In the end, Lee brought trouble on himself and the entire army. Even after he was released and in command of the Continental Army, he continued to insist on doing things his way. His wilfulness resulted in a military disaster at Monmouth in 1778, after which he was court-martialled.

If you constantly do things on your own terms at work, you could be courting danger of another kind – losing the confidence and respect of others.

Achievable steps can overcome impossible obstacles.

I can do everything through him who gives me strength.

Philippians 4:13

'What do you think,' Thomas Edison was once asked, 'is the first requisite for success in your field or any other?'

The great inventor replied, 'The ability to apply your physical and mental energies to one problem incessantly, without growing weary.'

In the workplace, many people run into problems in a project, so they spurn Edison's wisdom and set the project aside and turn to another. They exercise expedience.

Determination, conversely, is the quality that enables a person to resolve, 'I'm confident this is the right direction. I'm going to make it work!'

Determination is the choice to press ahead, no matter what obstacles appear. There is always a way. The appearance of obstacles should not be a surprise to any of us. Remember, the very laws of nature warn us that 'for every action there is an equal and opposite reaction'. Any movement will meet with some measure of friction.

So, you should expect obstacles and resistance, but don't let them stop you from accomplishing what you know needs to be done. Determination is the power to climb over obstacles. An accomplished mountain climber was once asked, 'How did you ever conquer that huge peak?'

'By putting one foot ahead of the other,' he replied.

You must look *into* words, as well as *at* them.

He will fill your mouth with laughter and your lips with shouts of joy.

Job 8:21

Signs Seen on Office Bulletin Boards and Cubicles

- Sure, but what about MY needs?
- No true act of logic ever goes unpunished.
- Just so you'll know, I don't work here.
- I was sure I made a mistake once, but I was wrong!
- This line for chump work.
- Is there anything else you can do for me today?
- If I throw a stick, will you leave?
- Well, this day was a total waste of makeup.
- I'm trying to imagine you with a personality.
- Errors have been made. Others will be blamed.
- A cubicle is just a padded cell without a door.
- I'm sure I forgot to remember something . . .
- Nice cologne. Must you marinate in it?
- Whatever kind of look you were shooting for, you missed.
- Corporate Suburbia: where they tear out the trees, then name streets after them.
- You! Off my planet!
- Let's see. Your ill-informed, crybaby opinion would be . . .?
- Some days, it's barely worth chewing through the rawhide straps and coming to work.

People who wish to know about the world must learn about it in its particular details.

Let the wise also hear and gain in learning.
Proverbs 1:5 NRSV

An ancient Arabian tale: An old dervish (monk) encountered two anxious merchants. 'You have lost a camel!' the dervish called.

'Indeed we have,' they replied, puzzled.

'Was he not blind in his right eye and lame in his left leg?' asked the dervish.

'He was,' the men responded.

'Had not your camel lost a tooth, and was he not loaded with honey on one side and corn on the other?'

'He was,' the merchants remarked. 'Please take us to him immediately.'

The dervish frowned, 'I have never seen your camel.'

'Certainly you have!' shouted the angry merchants. 'You shall answer before the *cadi* (magistrate).'

Before the *cadi*, the dervish explained, 'I knew I had crossed the tracks of a stray camel because I found no human footprints. I knew the animal was blind in one eye because it had cropped the vegetation on one side of the path, but not the other. I perceived it was lame in one leg from the faint impression made by one foot in the sand. I concluded the animal had lost a tooth because a small tuft of herbage remained uninjured wherever it grazed. As to the beast's burden, the ants informed me it was corn on one side and the clustering of flies that it was honey on the other.'

The *cadi* readily set the dervish free.

Nothing great was ever achieved without character.

For as he thinketh in his heart, so is he.

Proverbs 23:7 KJV

Inventor Thomas Edison had an intriguing way of celebrating his creative successes.

'During the summertime,' Edison said, 'after we had made something which was successful, I used to engage a brick-sloop at Perth Amboy and take the whole crowd down to the fishing banks on the Atlantic for two days.'

On one such excursion, Edison sat patiently with his fishing pole and line. But he hooked no fish. He continued fishing into the night. He continued the second day and also the second night. He was determined to catch a fish. But he failed. As they reached the end of their allotted time, Edison's companions urged him to put away his gear, so they could go home. But he would not. Finally, Edison's exasperated co-workers pulled up the anchor and sailed away, thus compelling him to stop.

Had Edison been the sole person making the decisions, he would have continued until he met his goal.

Edison's determination was woven into the very fibre of his being. He was determined in the lab, and he was determined on holiday. It was his character. Character is not merely a manner of behaviour you adopt at the office, then set aside at home. It is especially important for those in leadership to keep this principle constantly before them.

Give the world the best you have, and the best will come back to you.

Serve wholeheartedly, as if you were serving the Lord, not men.

Ephesians 6:7

A Letter to you from a V.I.P:

Dear Businessperson,

For now, I have chosen to be your customer. No matter what part of the organization you're in – no matter what job you perform – you are part of my customer service experience. You determine whether or not I'll be back.

When I call or visit your place of business, I expect to be treated well by the people who wait on me. But I judge your business by a lot more than just how I'm dealt with by the 'customer service people'. I look at everything. I ask questions: Is the facility clean and well maintained? Is the product or service of good quality? Did the shipment arrive on time and in good condition? Was the payment processing handled efficiently and correctly? Were the shelves well stocked and organized? Are written communications and phone messages clear and easy to understand? How long was I put on hold or passed from department to department?

Chances are, you'll never know me personally. You may never even see me. But you ought to appreciate me immensely. I am, after all, the reason your business exists – the reason you have a job. Do your part to make my experience a good one, and I'll be back to give you my hard-earned money.

Sincerely,

Your Customer

Before expecting obedience from others, a leader must learn to obey.

And this is love: that we walk in obedience to his commands.
2 John 1:6

Obedience is not a popular word in corporate settings. It is, however, one of the most critical character qualities and one that leadership must teach by example. The army has a saying: 'A senior must never regard his rank. The junior must never forget it.'

In other words, before leaders can expect obedience from those under them, they must maintain exemplary obedience to those over them. If your associates see you complaining about directives, they will immediately recognize your spirit of disobedience. Even if you comply with the directive, your attitude will provide justification for those under your leadership to balk at your instructions – and those of others in management.

The way to effectively teach obedience is to be even more obedient to your authorities than you expect others to be to you. Also, don't use your title or power to bully. Instead, earn respect through your knowledge, integrity and work ethic. Also, teach those within your leadership that corporate obedience is a matter of principal, a vital part of a company's dependability and productivity, as well as a measure of individual character.

If associates can't be depended on to do their jobs as instructed, the foundation of a company's goods and services is at risk. No company has achieved excellence through anarchy and disorganization.

’Tis not knowing much, but what is useful, that makes a wise person.

Do not boast about tomorrow, for you do not know what a day may bring forth.

Proverbs 27:1

A hard-working paste-up artist named Mark had worked for many years at a magazine. He was an expert with a knife, ruler and waxer machine as he carefully trimmed columns of copy and pasted them onto art boards to send to the printer. Mark read about the advent of desktop publishing and its effect on the magazine and book industries. The company offered to send him to college to learn the new technology, but he declined, convinced that he could still work faster and better than a computer-based artist.

The test came when Mark and his computer-based competitors were given 16-page sections of the magazine to produce. Those using the new technology produced quick, error-free work.

In his haste, Mark forgot to paste a key paragraph into one story and duplicated a sentence in another. When the waxer clogged, Mark knew he was in trouble.

While relieving him of his job, Mark's manager said sadly, 'Mark, you are like a great builder of covered wagons. Unfortunately, people today are driving comfortable cars powered by internal-combustion engines, not a team of mules.'

Mark is still looking for a publisher who appreciates old-style methods. He tells friends, 'I think this desktop publishing thing might just be a fad. Someday, publishers will need people like me again.'

We like Isaac Newton. He was a guy who understood the gravity of a situation.

Finally, brothers, whatever is true, whatever is noble, whatever is right, whatever is pure, whatever is lovely, whatever is admirable – if anything is excellent or praiseworthy – think about such things.

Philippians 4:8

Sir Isaac Newton wasn't the first person to be struck on the head by a falling apple or discern what causes objects to tumble towards earth. But there's a reason he's credited with discovering the theory of gravity. He agonized over the phenomenon later known as gravity.

He calculated and hypothesized. In 1687, his famous *Principia* went to press and radically changed humanity's understanding of the universe. The ability to think and concentrate is what turns inspiration into discovery and practical application.

Here are a few tips to build your brain to Newtonian levels:

- The brain is like a muscle. Exercise it by picking a topic and contemplating it thoroughly. Don't discard the topic when you get stuck for answers. That's like putting down a barbell every time it begins to feel a little heavy.
- Imagination builds creativity. Feed your imagination by reading great books, viewing fine artwork or watching innovative films or TV programmes.
- Record your thoughts. This will keep you focused – and stop you forgetting key ideas and insights.
- Crossword puzzles, memory game, and word searches are great ways to challenge and develop your mind.
- If you need a break from all the thinking, rest your mind and enjoy an apple. Isaac Newton would approve.

Life is what we make it, always has been, always will be.

Do not fear, for I am with you; do not be dismayed, for I am your God.

Isaiah 41:10

A young couple hired a carpenter to help them restore an old farmhouse. During a rough first day on the job, a flat tyre made him lose an hour of work, his electric saw broke and, finally, his ancient truck refused to start when it was time for him to go home.

While the couple drove him home, the carpenter sat in stony silence. On arriving, he invited them in to meet his family. As the threesome walked towards the front door, the carpenter paused briefly at a small tree, touching the tips of the branches. As he opened the door to his home, he underwent an amazing transformation. His tanned face relaxed. He smiled as he hugged his two small children and kissed his wife.

Afterwards, he walked the couple to their car. They passed the tree, and the husband asked, 'Why did you touch the tree like that earlier?'

'Oh, that's my trouble tree,' the carpenter replied. 'I can't help having troubles on the job, but troubles don't belong in our home. So I hang them up on the tree every night. In the morning, I pick them up again.' He smiled, 'Funny thing though, when I come out in the morning, there aren't nearly as many as I remember hanging up the night before.'

A wise person hears one word and understands two.

The fear of the LORD *teaches a man*
wisdom, and humility
comes before honour.
Proverbs 15:33

When Congressmen for the seceding southern states formed the Confederate States of America, they chose US Senator Jefferson Davis to be their leader. Little did Davis realize that the clerical assistant who faithfully worked for him would be remembered as a hero for generations.

Robert E. Lee, an experienced soldier, had been confined to a desk in Richmond, Virginia. There he obediently carried out the president's instructions without complaint. It was not until June of 1862, more than a year after the fighting began, that Lee entered the battlefield.

Although history has demonstrated Lee to be the superior strategist, he deferred to Davis and regularly cleared his plans with Davis before implementing them. With Lee's leadership in the field, the Confederate army repelled its enemy for the first time and began invading northwards.

It was written of Lee: 'He possessed every virtue of the great commanders, without their vices. He was a foe without hate; a friend without treachery . . . a neighbour without reproach; a Christian without hypocrisy . . . He was a Caesar without his ambition; a Frederick without his tyranny; a Napoleon without his selfishness; and a Washington without his reward. He was obedient to authority as a servant, and loyal in authority as a true king [yet] submissive to law as Socrates.'

Take laughter home,
and make a place in
your heart for it.

My soul shall be joyful in the LORD.
Psalm 35:9 KJV

Irrefutable Principles of Business Life

- A clear conscience should never be confused with a bad memory.
- Sweeping the room with a glance doesn't qualify as tidying one's work space.
- Letting it all hang out at work is unwise; you might not be able to get it tucked back in.
- Age is a very high price to pay for maturity.
- A closed mouth gathers no foot.
- Invoices travel through the mail at twice the speed of cheques.
- Whine doesn't improve with age.
- Experience is a wonderful thing. It enables you to recognize a mistake when you make it again.
- A consultant who thinks logically provides a nice contrast to the real world.
- Just when you start to win the rat race, scientists will develop bigger, faster rats.
- Jumping to conclusions, running your mouth, and ducking responsibility don't count as fitness exercises.
- It is better to light one small candle than to be seen with no makeup under fluorescent lighting.

Take time to enjoy life today – or at least very soon. For you never know how soon it will be too late.

He gives power to the tired and worn out, and strength to the weak.

Isaiah 40:29 TLB

Consider this: In Western Europe, paid holidays are typically four to six weeks for all regular workers. In Holland, for example, civil servants are entitled to roughly nine weeks of paid holiday – and the government adds a bonus to workers' salaries to help ensure that they have enough money to take a proper holiday.

In contrast, the US has no official vacation policy. Employers are not required to provide them, and the starting norm is only two weeks. Millions of the hard-working poor, without steady employment, have no paid vacation. And millions of the hard-working well-to-do have decent vacation plans that they are unable to take full advantage of because of the excessive demands of their positions. Further, Americans are much more likely to keep working while on vacation – especially in this age of mobile phones and laptop computers.

The Western Europeans have come to understand that being a good, hard-working employee requires an annual period of serious relaxation. Not just a three-day weekend now and then, but a genuine unwinding. If you are a manager, realize the time needed for workers to renew themselves mentally, physically and spiritually. If you aren't in management, try to take the holiday time you do have – and use it wisely and restfully.

Peace of mind is nearer when we laugh than when we fret.

A cheerful mind works healing.

Proverbs 17:22 AMP

More Signs Seen on Office Bulletin Boards and Cubicles

- My boss is a travel agent for guilt trips.
- Next mood swing: eight minutes.
- And your point would be?
- Of course I don't look busy; I did it right the first time.
- Do not start with me. You will not win.
- You have the right to remain silent. Feel free to exercise it.
- All stressed out and no one to pummel.
- I'm one of those bad things that happen to good people.
- How can I miss you if you won't go away?
- I do marathons, and I do meetings. I don't do marathon meetings.
- Don't upset me. I'm running out of places to hide the bodies.
- You interrupt my break; I break your pencil.
- Let's compromise: you do it my way, and I'll do it my way.
- Peace at any price – as long as you're paying.
- I always give 100 per cent at work: 7 per cent on Mondays, 23 per cent on Tuesdays, 47 per cent on Wednesdays, 19 per cent on Thursdays, 5 per cent on Fridays.
- Please keep your voice down; I'm trying to sleep!

Sticks in a bundle are unbreakable.

Two are better than one, because
they have a good return for their work:
If one falls down, his friend can help
him up. But pity the man who falls
and has no one to help him up!

Ecclesiastes 4:9–10

The Lone Ranger was misnamed. He wasn't 'Lone' at all. He didn't defeat the bad guys or escape from danger by himself. He had the help of his faithful friend, Tonto, not to mention his fast and trusty horse, Silver. Human beings just aren't designed to conquer life on their own. Whether it's figuring out a new software program, moving heavy office furniture or coping with depression on the job, some situations require a call for help.

You might be one of those people who has trouble asking for help. If so, just remember that the assistance you need is available, regardless of whether it's physical, emotional, financial or technical. It may take a little research and vulnerability to connect with the right counsellor, friend, co-worker or family member, but sending up an S O S when you need it is a sure sign of maturity – not weakness. Finding the support or guidance you need can make a great difference in the way you work, the way you think about your job and, perhaps most important, the way you live outside work.

Don't be afraid to reach out when you need a lifeline. And remember, the person you seek help from today might be the one who needs your expertise, guidance or moral support somewhere down the road.

The human heart has hidden treasures, in secret kept, and silence sealed.

Set a guard over my mouth, O Lord; keep watch over the door of my lips.

Psalm 141:3

One of the primary characteristics of a valued co-worker is the ability and determination to keep confidences. 'Why' is simple. Trust is a key factor in every relationship. People want a friend, a colleague, with whom they can feel safe. In fact, the word confidential is derived from the same root word as confidence. If you can keep a confidence, people will have confidence in you.

So learn to put a lock on your lips and keep secrets – secret! When you encounter the compulsion to whisper what you've been told to someone else (and you will), remember that trust builds relationships, but betrayal tears them apart. Your peers, your managers and those you lead will respect you, value you and know they can depend on you when you prove you are trustworthy in the safekeeping of confidential matters. This respect and value can only serve to enhance your position in your job.

Certainly, if someone is planning to do something illegal or harmful to himself or herself or to other people, you must exercise discretion as to what is the greater good – breaking a confidence or letting harm come to someone. But, for the most part, confidential matters belong in a vault to which only you have the key. It's a key of trustworthiness, hanging from a key chain of sound judgment.

Doubt indulged soon becomes doubt realized.

It is God's will that by doing good you should silence the ignorant talk of foolish men.
1 Peter 2:15

A group of frogs was hopping through the woods. Suddenly, two of them plunged into a deep pit. As the other frogs circled the pit, they quickly concluded that their amphibious friends were doomed. Frantically, the two unfortunate frogs began leaping with all their strength. 'Give it up,' some of their cohorts scolded them. 'You are as good as dead.'

Still, the two frogs kept jumping.

After half an hour, one of the trapped frogs became discouraged, curled up in a dark corner of the pit and waited to die. But the other kept jumping, even though its companions continued to jeer. Finally, with one mighty lunge, it leaped to the rim of the pit and pulled itself to safety.

'Wow, what a hop!' one of the negative frogs commented. 'I guess it was a good thing you ignored us.'

The now-safe frog simply looked at it companions with a puzzled expression on it green face. Then, through a series of frog sign-language gestures, it explained to the others that it was deaf. It didn't hear their discouraging words. And, in fact, when it had seen their frantic gestures, it assumed they were encouraging it!

The lesson: you can accomplish amazing feats when you turn a deaf ear (or two) to the discouraging words of negative-thinking naysayers.

Whatever you are, be a good one.

Commit to the LORD whatever you do, and your plans will succeed.

Proverbs 16:3

Suggestions for Business Success

- Find a job you love. This alone will determine 90 per cent of your career happiness.
- Be wise always as to how you spend your time and your talent.
- Give people more than they expect – and do so cheerfully. Be the most positive, encouraging and kind-hearted person you know.
- Be forgiving towards others and towards yourself. No one is perfect.
- Be generous, and not just with money.
- Cultivate a grateful heart.
- Be persistent about developing and exercising persistence.
- Discipline yourself to save money, regardless of your financial woes. Don't wait till the 'next raise' to start saving.
- Treat everyone just as you want to be treated.
- Determine that you will constantly improve on your skills and learn new ones. Commit yourself to quality.
- Understand that happiness isn't based on titles, salary or possessions.
- Be loyal. Be honest. Take good care of those you love.
- Be a self-motivated, self-starting person of action.
- Be decisive. Some decisions won't turn out the way you hope, but indecision rarely leads to anything good.
- Stop blaming others. You are responsible for your life, your happiness, and your well-being.
- Be courageous. You don't want to look back on your life someday and live with the regret of what might have been.
- Don't do anything that wouldn't make your mum and dad – or your children – proud of you.

Good words are worth much.

It is not good to have zeal without knowledge, nor to be hasty and miss the way.
Proverbs 19:2

Don't think you have time or money to edit and proofread that business letter, advertisement, Web site or brochure? Think again as you consider the following facts from a communications briefing presentation:

- Twenty-three per cent of all business and government communications is generated to provide clarification – or seek clarification – about reports, letters and memos that weren't clearly written in the first place.
- Citibank cut its staff training time in half by revising a business form so that customers and employees could better understand it.
- Mistakes in copy cost US businesses billions of dollars each year. For example, one firm had to send 60,000 follow-up letters to clarify a poorly-written business piece it had sent to its clients. Another firm had to completely re-do a major marketing mailing because its phone number was incorrect in a mailing that went out to thousands of potential and current customers.
- The average business communication piece has at least fifteen useless words.

Editing is well worth the effort to ensure that your business communication is clear, correct and concise. If you don't have a skilled editor on staff, consider a top-notch freelance professional. After all, consumers can't respond to your communication if they get the wrong message or don't know what you are trying to say.

If you want to be truly great, be great in the eyes of a child.

Do not exasperate your children; instead, bring them up in the training and instruction of the Lord.

Ephesians 6:4

The *Home Alone* movies made light of a child being accidentally left without adult supervision. Comic events ensued, no one got hurt (except for the bumbling bad guys), and everyone had a few good laughs.

In the real world, however, too many children are left home alone. And the dangers they face are real. According to a national survey of working parents conducted by the *Tulsa World*, one in five children aged six to twelve is regularly left without supervision after school. Thirty-five per cent of ten- to twelve-year olds care for themselves until their parents come home from work. And cost is not the main factor. Affluent working parents leave their children home alone as much or more than less well-off parents do. Child-care advocates warn that any time children spend unsupervised is filled with danger: drug or alcohol use, injury, crime and falling behind in studies.

If you are a working parent, consider your child's welfare carefully before making 'home alone' an option. Investigate day-care or flexible work hours. Or, consider a school – or church-related extracurricular activity that provides kids late-afternoon supervision.

It's true that after-school care can be expensive and complicated. But aren't the expense and effort well worth it? *Home Alone* might make an entertaining movie premise, but it's no way to raise healthy, safe kids.

The most wasted day is that in which we have not laughed.

There is a right time for everything . . . A time to laugh.
Ecclesiastes 3:1,4 TLB

A corporate Managing Director held a retreat for his staff in the. When they arrived, the MD asked them to assemble down by the lake. 'Resort officials have stocked this lake with a couple of hundred piranha,' he told them. 'They were reluctant, but I made it worth their while. I want to determine the most courageous people on my team by offering £1,000 to anyone brave enough to swim across.'

Moments passed. Staff members whispered to each other and shook their heads. Then suddenly, a young woman plunged into the water. With screams of terror, she began swimming madly across the lake. At last, she reached the far shore and pulled herself to safety. Her clothes were torn. She was covered with bite marks.

The entire staff raced around the lake and gathered at her side. 'You see? I knew there was one brave soul among all you cowards,' the MD pontificated. 'Jennifer here is now £1,000 richer. Jennifer, is there anything you would like to say to the group?'

Slowly, Jennifer struggled to her feet. 'Yes,' she said, 'I have four words I would like to say.'

'Very well,' the MD responded. 'Everyone, listen to brave Jennifer's four important words.'

With that Jennifer faced the staff, cleared her throat, and screamed, 'WHO PUSHED ME IN?'

We know purity, not only by reason and law, but also by the heart.

Set an example for the believers in speech, in life, in love, in faith and in purity.

1 Timothy 4:12

In the workplace, there is one topic more sensitive than politics or religion: sexual harassment. To some, it's merely a nuisance – something that has cast a pall of uneasiness over office banter. But to its victims, sexual harassment is a real threat that destroys careers and friendships – and sometimes entire companies.

In America, one company's employee manual states that the average monetary award in a sexual harassment case is $237,660. The average cost a company incurs to defend such a case is $300,000. And these costs are just the beginning.

A study by *Working Woman* magazine revealed that the typical Fortune 500 company loses $6.7 million a year in absenteeism, employee turnover, low morale and decreased productivity related to sexual harassment. But the most serious casualties are the women (and quite often men) who suffer with anger, fear, anxiety, humiliation and alienation at the hands of this corporate scourge, as well as a variety of health problems, including insomnia, eating disorders and acute depression.

Don't let sexual harassment be part of your work environment. Choose your words carefully. Be careful about the nature and tone of stories or jokes. When in doubt, DON'T. Be respectful of varying individual comfort levels with things like hugs and pats on the back.

And if there's any doubt – hands off.

The ability to delegate is a busy person's wealth.

I know your eagerness to help, and I have been boasting about it.

2 Corinthians 9:2

Often in business, the independent, self-reliant entrepreneur is revered. Such people live by adages like 'If you want something done right, you have to do it yourself'. Being responsible for your actions is certainly admirable, as is the ability to get things done without forming a committee. However, it's important not to overlook the wisdom and efficiency of delegating.

Thomas Edison, for example, is viewed by many as a lone genius, toiling away in his laboratory. In reality, he was not a hermit-inventor. He kept a large team working on as many as forty-five inventions at a time.

This system required expert management and precise scheduling. 'We had all the way from 40 to 50 men,' Edison said of his system. 'They worked all the time. Each man was allowed from four to six hours sleep.' While Edison's work schedule was a bit harsh, his principle is sound. One man simply couldn't have managed 45 or 50 inventions and experiments simultaneously.

If you are willing to share your knowledge and enthusiasm, you can build a delegation of key people who can help you complete more work in a shorter time span. You will probably find that your co-workers appreciate your trust in them- and the opportunity to learn new skills, especially if you allow them more sleep than Edison did.

Always do right.
This will gratify
some people and
astonish the rest.

Let the wise listen and add
to their learning.
Proverbs 1:5

Keys for Adding Life to Work

- Appreciate the value of time. Grab it, use it well, and savour every moment of it.
- Remember that it's easier to prevent bad habits from forming than it is to break them once formed.
- As you drive the road to success, consider letting others travel with you. The trip will be more fun.
- You should have a good reason for speaking out; you don't necessarily need a good reason for remaining silent.
- Of all the items you can wear to work, your facial expression is the most important.
- Avoid being paranoid or overly sensitive.
- Receive both praise and constructive criticism with grace.
- Be bold in what you stand for. Be careful what you fall for.
- Never give up on miracles. They do happen.
- Don't rain on other people's parades. Only a drip would do that.
- Don't postpone joy.
- Find ways to truthfully compliment co-workers on a job well done.
- Get real!
- Choose to give co-workers the benefit of the doubt.
- Applaud the achievement of others.
- Don't forget to say 'Thank you!'

Sometimes, all you get from working your fingers to the bone is bony fingers.

I know the best thing we can do is to always to enjoy life.

Ecclesiastes 3:12 CEV

American workers can be called many things, but 'lazy' isn't one of them. According to researcher/writer Brian Robertson, middle-earning workers in the US – those earning $50,000 or more a year work an average of fifty hours a week. Small-business proprietors have it even tougher. Their average work week consists of sixty hours.

Robertson also uncovered another interesting statistic. What sector of the American work force is most devoted to the job? The answer may surprise you – working mothers married to high-earning husbands.

It's time for America to re-examine its priorities and re-evaluate how much money is 'enough'. Our children don't really care about the size of our portfolios or our titles. They want and need time with their parents and grandparents.

Consider how you might invest those extra ten or twenty hours you spend at work every week. What could they mean to your child, your friend, your spouse or your health? Maybe it's time to make something other than your career the first priority in your life.

Those drivers on their cell phones really annoy me. I'd pull alongside them and give them a piece of my mind – if I weren't so busy putting on my makeup.

Know also that wisdom is sweet to your soul; if you find it, there is a future hope for you, and your hope will not be cut off.

Proverbs 24:14

The mobile phone has become an invaluable tool for many businesspeople. It increases one's availability and dramatically heightens the productivity of time spent in traffic jams, waiting in airports and so on. It is also handy in emergency situations, whether the emergency is a flat tyre on the motorway or a last-minute change to a company report.

However, this popular item also has drawbacks. For example, did you know that holding a cell phone next to your head exposes you to high levels of electromagnetic radiation?

Scientists haven't determined if this radiation is harmful, but some doctors recommend using caution. After all, can electromagnetic radiation directed to our skulls be beneficial? One alternative is using a mobile phone headset combination, which dramatically reduces exposure to radiation, according to *Men's Health* magazine.

These phones pose another risk as well. Studies indicate that handheld mobile phones slow drivers' reaction times by up to one second and increase the likelihood of having an accident by a factor of nine!

Be prudent about when and where you use your mobile phone. Your head (and the rest of your body) will thank you.

The largest room in the world is the room for improvement.

Lazy hands make a man poor,
but diligent hands bring wealth.
Proverbs 10:4

TV producer Sherwood Schwartz was frustrated. He had created a television show that he felt was a winner. However, network executives from CBS had shown the pilot programme to test audiences, who were unimpressed by the show's content and attempts at humour.

Some producers give up and move on to the next idea when faced with such rejection, but Schwartz believed that his idea, while admittedly campy and silly, had merit. So he tinkered with his show, re-writing scenes and replacing characters. He replaced a cutesy character named Bunny, for example, with a wholesome farm girl named Mary Ann.

Schwartz's reworked show was a hit with test audiences. In 1964, it made its network debut and immediately garnered a host of delighted fans. More than thirty years later, *Gilligan's Island* is still showing, thanks to its popularity in the syndication market.

It doesn't take a professor to realize that you shouldn't cast away your ideas merely because the business climate is getting rough. Be willing to make a few changes or approach from another angle. Then, launch out with courage. Even something that seemed like a shipwreck at first could make you a Skipper (CEO), a Millionaire, or a Movie Star.

Where our work is,
there let our joy be.

Never tire of doing what is right.

2 Thessalonians 3:13

Long ago there were two jars. Each was carried by a king's waterbearer on opposite ends of a long pole. One jar was perfectly made, with no cracks or chips. The other jar was unglazed earthenware – with a crack at its base.

Daily, the waterbearer would walk to the river and fill both containers, then carry them to the king's palace. Once inside, the first jar offered its full contents into the king's cistern. The other had less to offer since its water had leaked through the crack on the way.

Despondent, the cracked jar pleaded with the waterbearer, 'Please, sir, replace me. I am a failure. I spill so much that my offering cannot compare to what the perfect jar brings. I'm ashamed!'

The waterbearer smiled. 'Take a look at the hill we climb each day.' The jar obeyed. All along the path bloomed beautiful wildflowers. 'I've been planting seeds as I walk up the hill,' said the waterbearer. 'And those flowers you see now have grown from your loss, little jar. Flowers that please the king and all his people.'

Like the jar in this folk tale, if you do your job diligently, you will be able to survey the landscape and see the flowers of faithfulness that you have grown. Not because you are perfect, but because you were faithful to your task.

Perspective is everything. What looks like a monster through the magnifying glass is only a harmless house spider to the naked eye.

A happy heart is good medicine.

Proverbs 17:22 AMP

One day in an office building, the whir of routine activity was shattered by screams of terror. Associates became frantic, grabbing their personal belongings and rushing for the exits, for at the main entrance stood the devil himself in all his imposing terror.

The Prince of Darkness laughed derisively as he watched the fearful panic exploding before his gleaming eyes. One person, however, was undaunted. A silver-haired man near retirement age typed quietly and dutifully in his cubicle, seemingly unaware of the frenzy around him.

Nonplussed, the devil strode toward the elderly gentleman. With great flourish, he cleared his throat and raised his pitchfork in the air. 'Old man,' he roared. 'Why don't you flee like the rest? Are you so old that you are unable to run? Or are you frozen in terror?'

The man looked up and answered calmly, 'Neither of the above.'

Shocked, the devil shouted, 'I don't understand you. Don't you know who I am?'

'Of course I know,' the man said evenly. 'You are the devil.'

'But why aren't you terrified of me, as all of your co-workers are?'

The man smiled slightly. 'Why should I be afraid of you? I've been working for your sister for the past thirty-two years!'

A boss is not a person to lean on, but a person to make leaning unnecessary.

'I have set an example that you should do as I have done for you.'

John 13:15

Ten Commandments for Building a Troubled Workplace

1. Give employees everything they want. That way, they'll come to believe that the world owes them a living.
2. When employees make inappropriate remarks, laugh at them. They'll think they're clever.
3. Don't train them or provide educational resources. Let them figure out things for themselves.
4. Avoid use of the word 'wrong'. It can create guilt complexes.
5. Do your staff's work for them whenever possible. After all, don't you want them to depend on you?
6. Fight with your peers in front of your staff. That way, they won't be too shocked when they hear you've been fired or disciplined.
7. Give them raises and bonuses whether they deserve them or not. After all, why should your people have it as tough as you did? Plus, denial can lead to frustration.
8. Always take your employees' side when customers or clients complain about them. After all, those 'outsiders' are probably prejudiced against your people.
9. Pamper employees with expensive meals, gifts, first-class flights, and hotel accommodation.
10. When they fail or get into trouble, apologize for yourself by saying, 'I don't know why this happened – I gave them everything they could possibly want!'

The greatest test of courage on earth is to bear defeat without losing heart.

Patience is better than pride.

Ecclesiastes 7:8

'I speak without exaggeration,' Thomas Edison once said, 'when I say that I have constructed three thousand different theories in connection with the electric light, each one of them reasonable and apparently likely to be true. Yet in two cases only did my experiments prove the truth of my theory.'

That means Edison developed 2,998 failed theories along with his two successful experiments! The story of the light bulb is a long, tedious tale of repeated trial and failure. Yet, through it all, Edison was watching attentively – and learning.

Another lesson can be learned from Edison: As various attempts to carbonize a cotton thread for a light-bulb filament failed, he had to exercise his determination with great patience while handling a fragile component. Indeed, the more intent a person becomes, the more patient he or she must be to keep from ruining the goal of earnest efforts.

So, follow Edison's lead. When failures mount, step back. Re-examine your goal. Then turn the raw energy of frustration into a renewed determination to keep striving towards that goal. Determination is a decision, not a feeling. It is a foundational principle of good character.

As you develop and test your own bright ideas, remember also to emulate Edison's patience. The combination of these two characteristics constitute a formula for unparalleled success.

One who stops being better stops being good.

Be very careful, then, how you live—not as unwise but as wise, making the most of every opportunity.

Ephesians 5:15–16

The ABCs of Building a Better Workplace

- Accept co-workers for who and what they are.
- Be kind and considerate.
- Create a positive, can-do atmosphere.
- Don't insult or demean.
- Encourage excellence.
- Forget about past wrongs done to you.
- Grow smarter and wiser.
- Hang around with positive people.
- Insist on smiling at everyone.
- Join clubs at your job.
- Know that work is only part of your life, not life itself.
- Laugh as often as possible.
- Move around daily. Don't become a cubicle potato.
- Nip jealousy in the bud.
- Open your mind to new ideas, new friendships.
- Pay next time you and a co-worker have lunch.
- Quit insisting on being right all the time.
- Reach out to an associate who is struggling.
- Stretch your abilities.
- Talk about your goals to those who can help you achieve them.
- Uncomplicate your life.
- Vindicate yourself by your upright conduct, not excuses.
- Wait to talk. Don't wait to listen.
- Xerox (or photocopy) a humorous quote and share it with someone.
- Yank hurtful, hateful words from your speech.
- Zero in on what you need most to accomplish, and do it!

Acknowledgments

The publisher would like to honour and acknowledge the following people for the quotes used in this book:

T.J. Bower (12,128), Anna Pavlora (14), Nancy Parker Bruminett (16), Robert Green Ingersoll (18, 308), Miguel De Cervantes (20), Glen Drake (24), Mark Twain (26,294), Russian proverb (28), Hippocrates (30), Taylor Morgan (32,40,238, 250,292,300), Will Rogers (34), Babe Ruth (38), Confucius (42), Mary Kay Ash (46), Charles Caleb Colton (48), Ralph Waldo Emerson (50,140,206), Benjamin Franklin (52), Charles Schwab (54), Thomas Edison (68,234), French proverb (74,144), Georg Hegel (78), Steve Prefontaine (80), Charles E. Hummel (84), William Shakespeare (86), Karl Barth (88), Wayne Gretzky (90), Darrell Royal (92), Walter Bagehot (96), Aldous Huxley (98), Drew Cody (102, 126, 304), Andrew Jackson (104), Phillip James Bailey (108), Abraham Lincoln (110,282), Sam Jennings (112), Billy Graham (114), Lance Armstrong (118), Tertullian (122,302), Mrs. A. J. Stanley (130), Victor Hugo (132), Edward Young (134), Winston Churchill (136), William Wordsworth (138), Jude Phelps (142, 220), Theodore Roosevelt (146,166), Morgan

Kent (152), Madeline Bridges (154,258), Henry Ford (156), Todd Jay (158,290), Jean Paul Richter (160), Joseph Joubert (162), Louis Pasteur (172), Henry Ward Beecher (174), Lord Chesterfield (176,214), Eleanor Roosevelt (178), Elbert Hubbard (182), Martin Luther King Jr. (186), Olivia Kent (192,210,256), Kent Taylor (196), Thomas Fuller, M.D. (204,236,262), Roy Disney (212), William James (218), Winfred Holtby (222), Charles Dickens (224), Andrew Carnegie (228), Samuel Johnson (230), Gelett Burgess (232), Samuel Butler (240), African proverb (244), American proverb (246,248, 272,274,284), Business proverb (252), Heraclitus (254), German proverb (260), Jedd Hafer, Todd Hafer (264), Grandma Moses (266), Yiddish proverb (268), Greek proverb (270), Kenyan proverb (276), Charlotte Bronte (278), Frances Harergal (280), Chamfort (288), Luke Cody (296), The Busy Woman (208), and Oliver Cromwell (310).

References

Acknowledgments

Most of the selections in this book are based on the experiences and research of the author, Todd Hafer. However, some have been adapted from previous editions in the *God's Little Devotional Book* series.

The author and publisher also wish to acknowledge the Reverend Del Hafer, Pastor Steve Thurman, and Chaplain Ron Hafer, whose stories and sermons inspired several of the readings in this book.

Other titles in the
God's Little Devotional Book series:

God's Little Devotional Book
God's Little Devotional Book for Fathers
God's Little Devotional Book for Mothers
God's Little Devotional Book for Women
God's Little Devotional Book for Students
God's Little Devotional Book for Teens
God's Little Devotional Book for Graduates
God's Little Devotional Book for Couples
God's Little Devotional Book for Teachers
God's Little Devotional Book for Parents
God's Little Devotional Book on Success
God's Little Lessons on Life